A HORSE OF WHITE CLOUDS

Don Burness is Professor of English at Franklin Pierce College, Rindge, New Hampshire 03461.

A HORSE OF WHITE CLOUDS:

Poems from Lusophone Africa

Selected and Translated

by

Don Burness

with foreword by

Chinua Achebe

Ohio University Center for International Studies
Monographs in International Studies

Africa Series Number 55
Athens, Ohio 1989

© Copyright 1989 by the
Center for International Studies
Ohio University

Library of Congress Cataloging-in-Publication Data

A Horse of white clouds: poems from Lusophone Africa / selected and
translated by Don Burness.
    p. cm.-- (Monographs in international studies. Africa
series; no 55
    Translated from Portugese.
    ISBN 0-89680-158-6
    1. African poetry (Portugese) -- Translations into English.
2. English poetry -- Translations from Portugese. I. Burness,
Donald. II. Series
PQ9906. 5. E5H67 1989
869. 1--dc20   89-32437
                                                                                                  CIP

ISBN 0-89680-158-6

For Gerald Moser

CONTENTS

	page
FOREWORD by Chinua Achebe	xi
ACKNOWLEDGEMENTS	xiii
INTRODUCTION	xv

Poems from SÃO TOMÉ AND PRÍNCIPE 1

    Caetano da Costa Alegre
        Maria 3

    Francisco José Tenreiro
        The Ballad of Mista Silva Costa 5
        Blues Fragment 7

    Marcelo Veiga
        Costa Alegre 11

Poems from ANGOLA 13

    Joaquim Cordeiro da Matta
        My Fate 15

    Geraldo Bessa Victor
        Note on a Shop in the Muceque 17
        That Old Mulemba 19

    Mário António
        My Black Grandmother 23
        Fado 27
        Evora 29

Agostinho Neto
  Departure of the Contract Worker 31
  The Massacre of Contract Workers
    on São Tomé 33
  We Must Return 37

António Jacinto
  Monte Gracioso 39
  Oh If You Could See Here Poetry That
    Does Not Exist! 41
  Memories and Longings 45
  The Rhythm of the Tomtom 47
  Remembering 49

Alda Lara
  Testament 51

Antero Abreu
  Camarada Comandante 53

Costa Andrade
  Poem on the Death of Agostinho Nego 55
  The River Cunene 57

Ernesto Lara Filho
  Question 59

Jofre Rocha
  Guerilla Fighter 63

David Mestre
  November is When 65

Arlindo Barbeitos
  A Man of Rain 67
  O Night Flower 69
  The Cloud Produced an Elephant 71
  In the Forest of Your Eyes 73

Carlos Pimentel
  Towards the Future 75

João Pedro
  Homecoming 77

Carlos Ferreira
  Hope 81

Poems from CAPE VERDE 83

Jorge Barbosa
  Brother 85
  Poem of the Sea 91
  Return 95
  Bon Voyage 97

Manuel Lopes
  Crioule 105
  Quay 107

Osvaldo Alcântara
  Poem of the Boy who had been Torpedoed 109
  Victim of Famine 111

Yolanda Morazzo
  Boats 113

Gabriel Mariano
  Letter from Abroad 115

Ovídio Martins
  Anti-Evasion 117

Onésimo Silveira
  Lemma 119

Corsino Fortes
  Mindelo 121

Arménio Vieira
  Lisbon - 1971 125

João Rodrigues
  Synopsis for a Return to Childhood 127

Luís Silva
  The Island and Europe 131
  The Emigrant's Son 133

Ana Júlia
  Emigrant 135

Poems from GUINÉ BISSAU 139

   Amílcar Cabral
      Ships Without Moorings 141

   Carlos d'Almada
      Silence 145

Poems from MOZAMBIQUE 147

   Noémia de Sousa
      Let My People Go 149

   Kalungano
      Where I Am 153

   José Craveirinha
      Black Protest 159
      Song of the Great Barge 161
      A Man Never Cries 163
      Cell I 165

   Rui Knopfli
      Mulatto 167

   Rui Nogar
      Elegy for Mamana Isabel 169

   Glória de Sant'Anna
      Poem on Rain 173

   Mutimati Barnabé João
      Day 7 175
      I, the People 177

   Jorge Rebelo
      Letter from a Combatant 179
      Liberty 181
      Josina 183

BIOGRAPHICAL NOTES 187

FOREWORD

In the past one decade and more Don Burness has made it his business to search out and present to us little known riches of African writing locked away in the Portuguese language. Now he has gathered a fine harvest of his labor of love in an impressive volume, and in doing it he puts us all in his debt.

A Horse of White Clouds demonstrates that Lusophone African writing is not a cute little appendage to modern African literature as our ignorance used to suggest. On many counts it deserves to be widely appreciated. Set beside the better-known writing in English and French, it may lay claim to seniority in years, a matter of some importance in Africa. The Angolan poem "My Fate" by Joaquim Cordeiro da Matta is dated 1879 and must be one of the earliest works of modern African literature in a European language. It dealt with colonial oppression five years before the Berlin Conference mapped Africa out for colonization, and reminds us of the five hundred years of Portuguese occupation of Angola—from Queen Nzinga to President Neto.

But Lusophone African literature has other claims to our attention. It has both consistency and great variety. The former derives from the long and squalid history of colonization itself and the struggle for freedom which must have seemed so unequal and so hopeless through long periods of that history.

But there is also confidence in this poetry—a confidence which is more than a certain historic sense in the face of racial oppression that victory will ultimately come, as in the poem "Liberty" by Jorge Rebelo. There is, even more importantly, an aesthetic confidence which enables many of the poets we encounter here to confront issues that more cowardly practitioners would flee from! We are told too frequently that poetry is not intended to carry the weight of social and political concerns, and here we find poets (good poets, not propagandists) who are willing to challenge themselves and their craft to do just that and refute the counsel to evasion and timidity.

But to complete the vibrant and liberating picture presented by this anthology we also have poetry which sings of love (like the beautiful homage of António Jacinto to Alda Lara; or of Alda Lara herself in "Testament" distributing her goods to an assortment of loved ones before her much too early death); there is even poetry that has the lightness and playfulness of clouds forming and dissolving and reforming again into strange or familiar animal shapes before a tropical rainfall.

A Horse of White Clouds is like a good, clean tropical downpour after a season of drought.

Chinua Achebe

ACKNOWLEDGEMENTS

I would like to thank Inge Moser, Virgínio Melo, Manuel Ferreira, Maria Moreira Ellen, Manuel Lopes, and The Union of Angolan Writers for providing me with information. To my wife Mary-Lou I am indebted for her honest criticism of the translations and for her typing. To my friend Gerald Moser I express my appreciation and gratitude for the many occasions on which he helped me by providing information and gently encouraging me to be more precise when I strayed too far from literal translations.

Several of the translations were originally published in *Okike, The Greenfield Review*, and *Modern Poetry in Translation: 1983*. Others first appeared in my book *Fire: Six Writers from Angola, Mozambique and Cape Verde* (Washington, D.C.: Three Continents Press, 1977). In some instances I have emended my original translations.

INTRODUCTION

I

I have not tried to include in this book all the important poets from the five African countries which Portugal colonized. I have translated sixty-six poems by forty poets who write in Portuguese. The poems originally appeared in books, literary journals, and newspapers. I have tried to include representative poets of excellence who individually and collectively reflect historical, political, cultural, and psychological dimensions of African experience both under Portuguese domination and since independence in 1975. I have not excluded any poet because of race, political point of view, or because he or she wrote in an earlier age. Each of the poets belongs to Africa. I do not share the view of some anthologists that a political litmus test should determine if a particular poet's voice should be heard. The sunbird, the weaver, and the hornbill sing their own songs.

Truth wears many masks. There exists a general tendency among anthologists to equate Lusophone African writing solely with the national struggles for independence and the subsequent need for nation building. Such a one dimensional view refuses to recognize the importance of poets writing before the modern age and to see the wonderful variety of themes and attitudes expressed by writers from Angola, Mozambique, São Tomé and Príncipe, Cape Verde, and Guiné Bissau. Certainly it is true that for over a century Lusophone African writers have embarked on a journey of discovery and at times of rediscovery of their own authentic African identity, an identity raped and pillaged by five centuries of contact with European colonizers. It is true that wars of liberation were fought before independence was won.

The Portuguese professed to assimilate those Africans who could think like other Portuguese in Lisbon or Coimbra or Porto. In 1936 the great Cape Verdean troika, Jorge Barbosa, Manuel Lopes, and Baltasar Lopes challenged the Portuguese view of Africa by launching the first issue of the journal *Claridade* (Clarity) in Mindelo, the beautiful capital of the island of São Vicente. Quite simply, *Claridade* declared that Cape Verde had its own soul, its own music, its own traditions, and that the ten lonely islands three hundred miles west of Senegal were not and did not wish to become carbon copies of Portuguese civilization. In 1948 Angolan writers rose up to challenge Portuguese control of their psyche by affirming that the popular and authentic African essence (not the fatuous exotic portraits of Africa) must be articulated and defended. This movement called itself "Vamos Descobir Angola" (Let us Discover Angola). When Portugal, unlike Britain and France, refused to grant independence to its African colonies in the late fifties and early sixties, the peoples from the African lands went to war in order to claim by force what for centuries Europeans had maintained by force. Poets writing during this period reflect these national struggles for liberation. In many instances the poets were active combatants in the wars.

It is important to realize, however, that although Cape Verde and Angola beat a similar drum, the rhythms are not always the same. Cape Verde is a Crioule society in which racial miscegenation has resulted in a general absence of racial hatred and a general tolerance. Certainly racial consciousness exists in Cape Verde but racial distrust is not in the air. In a society where perhaps over three quarters of the people are mulatto, race is not a dominant issue. Neither is race a dominant theme in Angolan writing; some of the outstanding Angolan writers are white. Among them is António Jacinto, whose collection of poems *Sobreviver em Tarrafal de Santiago* (Surviving in the Prison of Tarrafal on Santiago) won the prestigious Noma Prize in 1986. White Angolans fought side by side with their black Angolan brothers and sisters during the struggle for independence in the nineteen sixties and nineteen seventies up to 1974. They suffered in prisons; they died on the battlefield; they helped construct a victory. It is not important to identify a writer from Angola or Cape Verde by race and I choose not to do so. I have merely mentioned the case of Jacinto to make a point. But the white population of Angola constitutes just a small percentage and the theme of a Crioule society is not as pronounced in Angolan poetry as it is in Cape Verdean writing.

Cape Verde is poor; the islands are barren and emigration is often the only hope to overcome repeated droughts and a land that will not provide for the people who love it. Cape Verdean writers sing sadly, wistfully, gently of the sea that takes the Cape Verdean far from his beloved islands and yet the emigrant cannot be unfaithful to the beloved and cherished mother-friend-lover Cape Verde. In Cape Verde there is the "morna" the popular music-poetry that expresses in its soft lyricism the pain and love that dwell in the heart of the people. Even today the themes of poverty, emigration, the sea, the morna, echo in the lines of poets. Of course a militant poetry exists as well. When Ovídio Martins in his defiant poem of protest Anti-Evasão (Anti-Evasion) cries out "Não vou para Pasárgada" (I will not go to Pasárgada), his fists are raised; his head is held high. For Cape Verdean nationalists "I will not go to Pasargada" suggests a resolve not to be a coward, not to give in to Portuguese domination, not to buy the Portuguese credo of European superiority and African inferiority, not to surrender to fanciful dreams of illusory foreign paradises. For these writers "Pasargada" is a metaphor for an attitude of escapism.

In Cape Verdean poetry the lyrical element dominates. Amílcar Cabral, the revolutionary leader who wrote poems in his youth, sang songs of love for Cape Verde; his love songs were African for he saw the islands as children orphaned from the great African continent. There is love also in Corsino Fortes' celebration of Mindelo; there is always love in the words of Jorge Barbosa who identifies in the poem "Brother" with all Cape Verdeans who have left the islands to endure loneliness and often danger and separation from the happy dreams of youth. Simply put, Cape Verdean poetry is rooted in the Cape Verdean experience.

In Angola, the long war for independence necessitated a national consciousness. This is embodied in Agostinho Neto, the gentle militant who led the Popular Movement for the Liberation of Angola (MPLA) first to independence and later in 1975 to nationhood. Neto, the first President of free Angola and a poet of great distinction, wrote a poetry of combat. In fact, his collection of poems *Sagrada Esperança* (Sacred Hope) was awarded the Poetry of Combat Prize at the University of Ibadan in Nigeria in 1975. In socialist Angola Neto the leader is one of the people and the anonymous people are subjects worthy of literary treatment. The dead are honored. Elegies flower over their graves. I have included several of these by Antero Abreu, Costa Andrade, Jofre Rocha, and Arlindo Barbeitos. There are, however, various colors to these bouquets. Barbeito's style is tight; like traditional Japanese and Chinese poets, he presents a few images that suggest rather than assert an emotion or an event. Barbeitos' preference for indirection, even ambiguity, continues one direction in Angolan writing. Mário António writing in the 1950s is the father of this path and his followers include the journalist-poet David Mestre. However, much Angolan poetry, like the elegies of Costa Andrade and Jofre Rocha, is written in a direct, unambiguous language. Often such poems run the risk of becoming nothing more than political sloganism. The poets I have chosen escape this temptation. Angola also has its lyrical poets—Jacinto, Alda Lara, and Geraldo Bessa Victor.

Mozambique like Angola fought a protracted war and the shells from that war explode in the poems. Racism was more overt in Mozambique than in Angola and consequently even before the war for independence strident voices challenged the arrogance of Lisbon. Kalungano (pseudonym of Marcelino dos Santos, one of the leaders of the Front for the Liberation of Mozambique [FRELIMO]) Noémia de Sousa and José Craveirinha say "No" to Camões and the other gods of Portugal and say "Yes" to Marian Anderson, to Paul Robeson, and to blackness. This is a virile poetry, an angry chorus. Mutimati Barnabé João, like his Angolan compatriots, celebrates and honors the dead soldiers who fertilized the fields for independence. Jorge Rebelo pays tribute to Josina Machel, the militant young woman who died at the age of twenty-five.

A common theme in Mozambican poetry is the "magaiça" or mine worker who leaves his native land, leaves his village, leaves his wife and children to work exhausting hours in the mines of South Africa. A parallel can be found in the experience of Angola and Cape Verde where contract laborers go to São Tomé to work on the plantations, to work and work and in the end gain nothing. Agostinho Neto's "The Departure of the Contract Workers" and "The Massacre of Contract Workers on São Tomé" and Gabriel Mariano of Cape Verde in "Letter from Abroad" refer to this painful experience.

Mozambique's most forceful poet is José Craveirinha; his staccato rhythms pulse with life and energy. Yet Craveirinha has different voices and I

have chosen to include both poems of strident anger such as "Song of the Great Barge" and poems of gentle understatement like "Cell I."
Poets from São Tomé and Príncipe and Guiné Bissau merit attention. Because São Tomé and Príncipe were centers of exploitation, centers of racial cruelty, voices from these twin islands have been less than meek. Francisco José Tenreiro (1921-1963) in his volume *Ilha de Nome Santo* (Island with a Saintly Name) can be considered one of the early protest writers in Lusophone Africa. Inspired by the poets of the Harlem Renaissance, Langston Hughes and Countee Cullen, he marched with them on the long journey for the black man to reaffirm his pride in his blackness, his identity as a black man.

Guiné Bissau has produced only a few poets of note. I have included two poems, one by Amílcar Cabral the revolutionary leader of the African Party for the Independence of Guiné and Cape Verde (PAIGC) and a tribute to the assassinated Cabral by Carlos d'Almada. Cabral and Neto and Marcelino dos Santos are poet-politicians who have become symbols not only in their native lands but throughout Africa. Cabral and Neto have become ancestors whose voices and deeds must continue to be honored; they are ancestors not only of a family and village but of an entire people. Léopold Senghor of Senegal, and Julius Nyerere of Tanzania are similar examples of the felicitous phenomenon of the writer-politician in Francophone and Anglophone Africa.

II

I have chosen poets who sing gently sad songs and poets who cry out ululations of pain. I have included poets who confidently and at times angrily challenge Portuguese domination. I have chosen poets who are friends of understatement, who suggest rather than assert and I have chosen poets who feel that the times have called for blatant assertion. I have chosen poets who think in political terms and I have chosen poets who see the totality of human experience as appropriate fields for literature—lost dreams of childhood, spiritual love, erotic love, love for the rivers, mountains, clouds, and beautiful landscapes of Africa. Wherever possible I have noted the year in which the poem was written.

I have also presented an historical perspective. Wherever possible I have noted the year in which the poem was written. One can argue that Caetano da Costa Alegre (1864-1890) is the first black poet of excellence to produce a collection of written poetry in Lusophone Africa. His love sonnet "Maria" reflects an ambivalent racial attitude we find in nineteenth and early twentieth century writing from Pushkin's *The Negro of Peter the Great* to the novels of Nella Larsen in America. More overt disenchantment can be found in "My Fate" by the extraordinary Angolan poet, journalist, novelist, historian, and linguist Joaquim Cordeiro da Matta (1857-1894).

I have been faithful to the rhyme schemes of these nineteenth century poets as well as those twentieth century poets who choose to write in rhyme; I feel it is important to reproduce faithfully the form as well as the tone, the thematic content, the patterns of imagery, and the individual timbre of each poem. In one poem, Francisco Tenreiro's "Ballad of Mista Silva," I have tried to reflect the fact that the narrator is a peasant who uses occasional Crioule words and grammatical constructions in what is basically a poem written in Portuguese. To do this I have blended rhythms of the Afro-American community with more "standard" English. In an occasional translation I have not followed the exact pattern of rhyme because I ended up with a poem that lost too much of the flavor of the original. Cabral's "Ships Without Moorings" has many lines of just one or two word with much end rhyme. I was unable to reproduce this successfully in English.

I have not been a timid translator. I have chosen at times to change words, phrases, and expressions that just did not sound right in English. I have tried to be faithful to the heart and soul of the poems, but not to every literal word or phrase. To create rhymes and rhythm and tone demands a certain freedom of the translator and whatever successes or failures I may have achieved, I have been guided by love of the poems themselves and by my love of language.

Poems from SÃO TOMÉ AND PRÍNCIPE

MARIA

Caetano da Costa Alegre

> À Exma Sr.ª D. LAURA
>
> *Por veres meu rosto negro*
> *Tu me chamaste carvao...*
> *Não me admira: fui lenha*
> *No fogo desta paixao.*

És alva e fria,
Anjo mimoso,
Tal como um dia
Triste, invernoso!

Eu bem podia
Calor fogoso,
Que te aquecia,
Dar-te amoroso.

Mas tu não queres?...
(Como as mulheres
Teimosas são!)

Sofres o frio,
E de arrepio!
Tendo carvão!...

São Tomé and Príncipe

MARIA

Caetano da Costa Alegre

To the Most Excellent Dona Laura

On Seeing My Black Face
You called me coal...
I'm not surprised: I was wood
For the fire of your soul.

You are cold and white
My dear friend
Like the chill of winter's bite
That never seems to end.

Each day, each night
My love to you I send
With heat and light
Praying I don't offend.

I am the coal
To give warmth to your cold soul
But you don't love me back,
I always see your hair, your face
Images time does not erase.
Why was I born black?

São Tomé and Príncipe

ROMANCE DE SEU SILVA COSTA

Francisco José Tenreiro

«Seu Silva Costa
chegou na ilha...»

Seu Silva Costa
Chegou na ilha:
calcinha no fiozinho
dois moeda de ilusão
e vontade de voltar.

Seu Silva Costa
chegou na ilha:
fez comércio di álcool
fez comércio di homem
fez comércio di terra.

Ui!
  Seu Silva Costa
virou branco grande:
su calça não é fiozinho
e sus moeda não têm mais ilusão!...

THE BALLAD OF MISTA SILVA COSTA

Francisco José Tenreiro

"Mista Silva Costa
arrived on the island..."

Mista Silva Costa
arrived on the island:
tattered clothes
two bits of illusion
an' a desire to return home.

Mista Silva Costa
arrived on the island:
Yes, sir - he made lots a money in booze
an' he made lots off the people
an' he made lots buying land.

Man alive!
Mista Silva Costa
he big white man now:
he got nice clothes
and his money be no more an illusion!...

São Tomé and Príncipe

FRAGMENTO DE BLUES

A Langston Hughes

Francisco José Tenreiro

    Vem até mim
nesta noite de vendaval na Europa
pela voz solitária de um trompette
toda a melancolia das noites de Georgia:
    oh! mamie oh! mamie
    embala o teu menino
    oh mamie oh! mamie
    olha o mundo roubando o teu menino.

    Vam até mim
ao cair da tristeza no meu coração
a tua voz de negrinha doce
quebrando-se ao som grave dum piano
        tocando em Harlem:
        - Oh! King Joe
          King Joe
        Joe Louis bateu Buddy Baer
        e Harlem abriu-se num sorriso branco

Nestas noites de vandaval na Europa
Count Basie toca para mim
e ritmos negros da América
encharcam meu coração;
        - ah! ritmos negros da América
        encharcam meu coração!

São Tomé and Príncipe

BLUES FRAGMENT

For Langston Hughes

Francisco José Tenreiro

All the melancholy of nights in Georgia
comes to me
this stormy night in Europe
through the solitary voice of the trumpet:
Oh! mammy! oh! mammy
rock yo lil' chil'
Oh! mammy, oh! mammy
look at de world stealin' yo chil'.

Black woman - your sweet voice
reaches me in the sadness of my heart
which breaks at the sad sound of a piano
playing in Harlem:
 - Oh! King Joe
        King Joe
Joe Louis beat Buddy Baer
and Harlem laughed its white toothed negro laugh.

In these stormy nights in Europe
Count Basie plays for me
and black rhythms from America
inundate my heart;
 - ah! black rhythms from America
        inundate my heart!

São Tomé and Príncipe

      E se ainda fico triste
      Langston Hughes e Countee Cullen
          Vem até mim
      Cantando o poema do novo dia
              - ai! os negros não morrem
              nem nunca morrerão!

      ... logo com eles quero cantar
      logo com eles quero lutar
              - ai os negros não morrem
              nem nunca morrerão!...

                        1943

São Tomé and Príncipe

And if I still am sad
Langston Hughes and Countee Cullen
    Come to me
singing the poem of a new day
 - ai! The black man is not dead
    nor will he ever die!

...By and by with them I want to sing
by and by with them I want to struggle
 ai, the black man is not dead
   nor will he ever die!...

                                          1943

COSTA ALEGRE

Marcelo Veiga

Numa ilha do equador
Onde florescem palmas e cacoeiros
E têm murmúrios doces os ribeiros,
Nasceu um sonhador
Um visionário, asceta,
Alma branca, de flor,
Que o destino fadou e sagrou poeta.

Menino e moça ainda,
Como a ave que bate a asa esperta e linda
Mal pressente na voz primeiro canto,
Deixou um dia, rindo, sem um pranto,
A sua ilha que o sol afaga a alinda.

Alegre lhe chamaram;
Para a glória o fadaram,
P'ra triunfador nasceu,
Mas como a ave que pelo espaço corre
E, após primeiro trilo, cai e morre,
Costa Alegre morreu!

São Tomé and Príncipe

COSTA ALEGRE

Marcelo Veiga

On an island at the equator
Where palm trees and cocoa grow
And the brooks gently flow,
Was born a man of dreams
An ascetic, a seer,
A soul pure and white it seems,
A poet chosen by fate for us to hear.

While still a child awakened from sleeping,
Like a bird first beating its beautiful wings
And beginning to raise its voice to sing,
One day he left laughing and without weeping
His beautiful island caressed and embellished by the sun.

Alegre was his name;
He was destined for honor and fame,
He was born to triumph it was said
But like the bird that takes off to the skies
And after the first trill, falls and dies,
Costa Alegre was dead.

Poems from ANGOLA

Angola

A MINHA SINA

Joaquim Cordeiro da Matta

É sem norte a minha vida,
e n'um mar revôlta vivo;
escravo de dura lida
eu sou a tudo captivo;
atraz do ignoto corro,
e na lucta eu soffro, eu morro.

1879

Angola

MY FATE

Joaquim Cordeiro da Matta

Without a guiding star is my life,
Even though I travel on turbulent seas;
I am a slave who endures constant strife
and toil, and knows no respite or ease;
I live in a world where I can't get ahead,
I struggle, I suffer, and then I'm dead.

1879

Angola

APONTAMENTO NA QUITANDA DO MUCEQUE

Geraldo Bessa Victor

Na quitanda do muceque
de S. Paulo de Luanda,
o menino negro chupa sorvete,
o menino branco come quitaba,
ambos sorrindo, ambos cantando
A Maria Candimba, o Abril em Portugal.

E a minha alma de poeta
—alma mestiça, luso-tropical—
descobre acenos de Africa
no gesto do menino branco
e visões da Europa
no olhar do menino negro.

Angola

NOTE ON A SHOP IN THE MUCEQUE

Geraldo Bessa Victor

In the shop in the muceque[1]
of S. Paulo de Luanda,
a black child is sucking sherbet,
a white child is eating quitaba,[2]
both smiling, both singing
'Maria Candimba,' and 'April in Portugal.'

And my poet's soul
—a hybrid soul, luso-tropical—
discerns signs of Africa
in the gesture of the white child
and visions of Europe
in the look of the black child.

---

1. township, a Kimbundu word. 2. a sort of pasta

Angola

A VELHA MULEMBA

Geraldo Bessa Victor

Aquela velha mulemba . . .

Vieram homens armados
de catanas e machados,
duros de corpo e alma
(onde a bondade não medra),
mandados por alguém de coração de pedra,
—e assim, em nome da lei,
durrubaram e mataram
aquela velha mulemba,
velha rainha sem rei.

Não sofreram, não choraram;
so eu chorei!

Minha velha mulemba . . .
À sombra dela (eu era monandengue),
com outros meninos brincando,
eu ensaiei meus passos de massemba . . .
Tantas vezes ali deitei meu luando
e ali fiquei cochilanda.
à sombra da mulemba

Só eu chorei de saudade,
quando a vi, hoje, caída,
morta. Foi como se fosse
a morte da minha vida!

Angola

THAT OLD MULEMBA

Geraldo Bessa Victor

That old mulemba...

Men armed with machetes
and axes came,
hardened in body and soul
(where goodness is not sown)
ordered by someone with a heart of stone,
—and thus, in the name of the law,
they demolished and killed
that old mulemba,
old queen without a king.

They did not suffer, they did not cry:
I alone cried:

My old mulemba...
Under its shade (I was a kid),
playing with other children,
I tried a step of the massemba...
So many times I stretched out my mat
and there did sums
under the shade of the mulemba.

Alone I cried from the nostalgic yearning,
where today I saw it fallen,
dead. It was as if
it were the death of my own life!

Angola

Você, leitor, que me está lendo,
vai dizer-me asim, com espanto:
—Porque sofre você? Eu não entendo
o motivo do seu pranto.
Derrubaram cajueiro,
onde você comeu bom caju, tanto e tanto;
derrubaram embondeiro,
onde você comeu muita mucúa, no gozo;
derrubaram também tamarindeiro,
onde você comeu tamarindo gostoso . . .
Derrubaram essas árvores
que lhe deram sombra e fruto;
e você ficou na mesma como um bruto,
não sentiu então o dó
que tem da velha mulemba,
que só lhe deu sombra, so!-

Ninguém pode compreender
a dor da minha saudade,
isto que me faz sofrer!

Você, leitor, que me esta á ler,
queira notar esta verdade
que não me sai mais de lembrança:

—Uma vez, em criança,
puxei os bigodes do meu avô velho;
deu-me uma bofetada,
que minha cara negra ficou logo encarnada.
Pois, por muitos anos, eu andei puxando,
dia a dia, as barbas da velha mulemba,
nelas fiz balouço, fiquei balouçando;
e a velha mulemba não ficou zangada,
nunca me fez nada,
nem um só açoite, nem um só lamento,
senão a carícia das suas longas barbas
no meu rosto, no meu corpo, quando o vento
as beijava e fazia estremecer . . .—

Minha velha mulemba . . .
Ah, só eu sei o que me faz sofrer!

Angola

You, reader, who are reading me,
you are going to tell me with surprise:
Why do you suffer? I do not understand
the cause of your weeping.
They cut down a cashew-tree,
where you ate so many good cashew nuts:
they cut down a baobab,
where you savoured many mucuas;
they also cut down a tamarind-tree
where you ate the tasty tamarind.
They cut down those trees
that provided you shade and fruit;
and you remained like a beast,
you did not feel then the compassion
that you now have for the old mulemba,
that gave you nothing but shade!

No one can understand
the grief of my longing.
which causes me to suffer!

You reader who are reading me
please note this truth
which I can never forget:

—Once as a boy
I tugged at the mustaches of my old grandfather;
he gave a slap,
so that my black face turned red.
So, for many years, day after day,
I used to pull the branches of the old mulemba,
out of them I made a swing to play;
and the old mulemba never became angry,
never did anything to me,
not a single slap, not a single lament,
other than strokings of the long hair
on my face, on my body, when the wind
was kissing and shaking it...

My old mulemba...
Ah! I alone know what makes me suffer!

Angola

MINHA AVÓ NEGRA

Mário António

Minha avó negra, de panos escuros
da cor do carvão
Minha avó negra, de panos escuros
que nunca mais deixou.

Andas de luto,
Toda és tristeza

Heroína de ideias,
rompeste com a velha tradição
dos cazumbis, dos quimbandas.

Não chinguilas no óbito
Tuas mãos de dedos encarquilhados
tuas mãos calosas da enxada
tuas mãos que me preparam
mimos da nossa terra
(quitabas e quifututilas),
tuas mãos, ora tranquilas,
desfiam as contas gastas
de um rosário já velho.

Já não sabes chinguilar
não fazes mais que rezar.
Teus olhos perderam o brilho.
E da tua mocidade

só te ficou a saudade
e um colar de missangas.

Avózinha, às vezes
ouço vozes
que te segredam saudades
da tua velha sanzala

Angola

MY BLACK GRANDMOTHER

Mário António

My black grandmother in dark clothes
color of carbon
My black grandmother in dark clothes
which she never gave up.

You go in mourning.
All is sadness.

Heroine of ideas,
you broke the old tradition
of cazumbis and quimbandas.[2]

You no longer chinguilar[3] at funerals,
your hands with wrinkled fingers
your hands, hardened from the hoe
your hands which prepared
gifts from our land
(quitabas[4] and quifufutilas[5]),
your hands, tranquil now,
untwist the beads worn
for a rosary grown old.

You no longer chinguilar
all you do is pray.
Your eyes have lost their glitter.
And from your youth
you only kept nostalgia
and a necklace of missangas.[6]

Dear grandmother, at times
I hear voices
that whisper to you memories
of your old sanzala[7]

Angola

de cubata onde nasceste
das algazarras dos óbitas
dos sonhos do alambamento
que supunhas merecer.

E penso que
se pudesses
talves revivesses
as velhas tradições![3]

of the cubata where you were born
of ululations at funerals
of the deceitful temptings of the quimbanda
of the dreams of alambamento[9]
that you thought to deserve.

And I think
if you could
perhaps revive
the old traditions!

---

1. spirits (this and other Angolan words in the poem are from Kimbundu).
2. traditional healers. 3. commune with spirits. 4. a sort of pasta.
5. meal of ground manioc. 6. beads. 7. village. 8. hut. 9. bride price.

Angola

FADO

Mário António

Garganta, xaile garganta
O corpo molda-se em voz
E a voz sem corpo no ar!

Candeeiros destacam rostos
Mais rostos: os que pedem
Os que troçam, os que imploram
os que ameaçam...

Faces diferentes do amor:
De ancas largas, maternal,
De pequenos seios castos
Até o amor assexuado.

Da garganta às ancas
—Mil faces do amor
No movimento de um xaile—
Canta-se o fado.

Angola

FADO

Mário António

Throat, shawl, throat
The body molds itself to the voice
And the bodiless voice to the air!

Lamps reveal faces
More faces: those that beseech
those that mock, those that implore
those that threaten...

Different faces of love!
Large hips, maternal,
Small chaste breasts
Including asexual love.

From the throat to the hips
—A thousand faces of love
In the movement of a shawl—
the fado is sung.

Angola

EVORA

Mário António

Céu violeta, firmes estrelas.

Exsuda cal o tronco
sobre a terra rossa.

Um vinho doce lave
o sarro de borrego
em nossa boca.

Évora ao longe. Olivos!
Paredes brancas de luar.

EVORA

Mário António

Violet sky, fixed stars.

The trunk exudes lime
over the red earth

A sweet wine washes down
the lamb skin
in our mouths.

Evora from a distance. Olive tree!
White walls in the moonlight!

Angola

PARTIDA PARA O CONTRATO

Agostinho Neto

O rosto retrata a alma
amartanhada pelo sofrimento

Nesta hora de pranto
vespertina e ensanguentada
Manuel
o seu amor
partiu para S. Tomé
para lá do mar

Até quando?

Além no horizonte repentinos
o sol e o barco
se afogam
no mar
excurecendo
o céu escurecendo a terra
e a alma da mulher

Não há luz
não há estrelas no céu escuro
Tudo na terra é sombra

Não há luz
não há norte na alma da mulher

Negrura
Só negrura...

Angola

DEPARTURE OF THE CONTRACT WORKER

Agostinho Neto

A face mirroring the soul
wrinkled through suffering

At this bloody twilight hour of weeping
Manuel
her love
departed for São Tomé
beyond the sea

Until when?

Beyond the horizon
sun and boat
suddenly drown
at sea
darkening
the sky, darkening the earth
darkening the soul of the woman

There is no light
there are no stars in the dark sky
Everything on earth is shadow

There is no light
the north star does not dwell in the soul of the woman

Blackness
Only blackness...

Angola

MASSACRE DE SÃO TOMÉ

Agostinho Neto

(para a ilustre amiga Alda Graça)

Foi quando o Atlântico
pela força das horas
devolveu cadáveres
envolvidos em flores brancas de espuma
e do ódio incontido das feras
sobre sangues coagulados de morte

As praias se encheram de corvos e de chacais
em fomes animalescas de carnes esmagadas
na areia
da terra queimada pelo terror das idades
escravizadas em cadeias
ná terra chamada verde
que as crianças ainda chamam verde de esperança

Foi quando no mar os corpos se embeberam
de vergonha e sal
nas águas ensanguentadas de desejos
e fraquezas

Foi então que nos olhos em fogo
ora sangue ora vida
ora morte
enterramos vitoriosamente os nossos mortos
e sobre as sepulturas
reconhecemos a razão do sacrifício dos homens
pelo amor
e pela harmonia
a pela nossa liberdade
mesmo ante a morte pela força das horas

nas águas ensanguentadas
mesmo nas pequenas derrotas acumuladas para a vitória

Angola

THE MASSACRE OF CONTRACT WORKERS ON SÃO TOMÉ

Agostinho Neto

(for my illustrious friend Alda Graça)

It was when the Atlantic
coughed up corpses
wrapped in white flowers of spume
driven by time
and the rough beast of hatred
dancing with death's coagulated blood

Crows and jackals filled the beaches
in their animal hunger
devouring mounds of flesh
in the sands
of earth burnt by the terror of the years
made slaves in prisons
on this land of green hope
that children still know of
as a land green with hope

It was when the corpses drank their fill
of a sea of shame and salt
waters made bloody by desires
and weaknesses

It was then that with our eyes filled with fire
now with blood, now with life, now with death
we buried victoriously our dead
and over the graves
we recognized that these men were sacrificed
for love
for harmony
for our liberty
even before the dance of death driven by time
in blood waters
even in the small accumulated defeats on the way to our victory

Angola

Em nós
a terra verde de São Tomé
será também a ilha do amor.

1953

Angola

For us
the green land of São Tomé
will also be an island of love.

1953

Angola

HAVEMOS DE VOLTAR

Agostinho Neto

Às casas, às nossas lavras
às praias, aos nossos campos
havemos de voltar

Às nossas terras
vermelhas do café
brancas do algodão
verdes dos milharais
havemos de voltar

Às nosses minas de diamantes
ouro, cobre, de petróleo
havemos de voltar

Aos nossos rios, nossos lagos
às montanhas, às florestas
havemos de voltar

À frescura da mulemba
as nossas tradições
aos ritmos e às fogueiras
havemos de voltar

À marimba e ao quissange
ao nosso carnaval
havemos de voltar

À bela pátria angolana
nossa terra, nossa mãe
havemos de voltar

1960

Angola

WE MUST RETURN

Agostinho Neto

To the homes, to our tillage
to the beaches, to our fields,
we must return

To our lands
red with coffee
white with cotton
green with maize fields
we must return

To our wealth of diamonds
gold, copper, petroleum
we must return

To our rivers, our lakes,
to our mountains, to our forests
we must return

To the coolness of the mulemba
to our traditions
to the rhythms and to the fires
we must return

To the marimba and to the quissange
to our carnival
we must return

To the beautiful Angolan homeland
our land, our mother
we must return

We must return
to Angola liberated
to Angola independent

1960

Angola

MONTE GRACIOSO

António Jacinto

Para lá das grades
      do arame farpado
      do fosso
para lá do torreão
dos soldados, las guaritas, das sentinelas
    o Gracioso

feito o
—seco, fero, estéril monte—de Camões
    o Gracioso
a amplidão dos gaviões e xinxerotes
e a imaginação insubmíssel do poeta

Entre a terra e o céu
no píncaros do monte
tu Poesia, num halo de nuvem
varrida pelos ventos do Sara
tu Poesia
num aceno só para mim.

                                1966

Angola

MONTE GRACIOSO

António Jacinto

Beyond the gratings
        The barbed wire
        The trench
Beyond the turrets
The Soldiers, the sentry boxes, the sentries
        Gracioso

Called the
        "dry, fierce, sterile mountain" by Camôes
        Gracioso
The breadth of the sparrow hawks and xinxerotes
And the unconquerable imagination of the poet

Between earth and sky
Atop the pinnacle of the mountain
You Poetry, with a halo of clouds
Swept by winds from the Sahara
You Poetry
With a nod just for me.

1966

Angola

AH! SE PUDÉSSEIS AQUI VER POESIA QUE NÃO HÁ!

António Jacinto

Um rectângulo oco na parede caiada Mãe

Três barras de ferro horizontais Mãe
Na vertical oito varões Mãe
Ao todo
vinte e quatro quadrados Mãe
No aro exterior
Dois caixilhos Mãe
somam
doze rectângulos de vidro Mãe
As barras e os varões Mãe
projectam sombras nos vidros
feitos epelhos Mãe
Lá fora é noite Mãe
O campo
a povoação
a ilha
o arquipélago
o mundo que não se vê Mãe
Dum lado e doutro, a Morte, Mãe
A morte como a sombra que passa pela vidraça Mãe
A morte sem boca sem rosto sem gritos Mãe
E lá fora é o lá fora que se não vê Mãe

Cale-se o que não se vê Mãe
e veja-se o que se sente Mãe
que o poema está no que
                    e como se vê, Mãe
Ah! se pudésseis aqui ver poesia que nao há!
Mãe
aqui não há poesia
É triste, Mãe
Já não haver poesia
Mãe, não há poesia, não há
Mãe

Angola

OH IF YOU COULD SEE HERE POETRY THAT DOES NOT EXIST!

António Jacinto

One empty rectangle, a whitewashed wall, Mother
Three horizontal iron bars Mother
With eight vertical bars, Mother
In all
Twenty-four squares, Mother
In the external ring
Two window frames Mother
Contain
Twelve rectangles of glass, Mother
The bars, Mother
Project shadows on the glass
Made mirrors, Mother
There outside it is night, Mother
The countryside
The town
The island
The archipelago
The world that cannot be seen, Mother
From one side to another, Death, Mother
Death like a shadow that passes through the window-pane
Mother
Death without a mouth, without a face, without screams,
Mother
And there outside is an outside that can't be seen, Mother
What one doesn't see remains silent, Mother
And one sees that one feels, Mother
A poem is found in what and in how we see, Mother
Oh if you could see here poetry that does not exist!
Mother
There is no poetry here
It is sad Mother
No longer to have poetry
Mother, there is no poetry, none
Mother

Angola

Num cavalo de nuvens brancas
o luar incendeia carícias
e vem, por sobre meu rosto magro
deixar teus beijos Mãe, teus beijos Mãe

Ah! se pudésseis aqui ver poesia que não há!

1968

Angola

Riding a horse of white clouds
The moon on fire removes shrouds
Bringing to my pale and listless face
Kisses, Mother from you, kisses
Oh, if you could see here poetry that does not exist!

1968

Angola

SAUDADES

António Jacinto

No paisagem a Ilha do Fogo é presenca.

Ao—desamparinho—da tarde
Os coqueiros são lento adeus

A vela no mar
escreve em geometria de espuma
              —partida de quem fica
E as nuvens ao sopro incessante vão
dos alísios mandos
              —viagem de quem não partiu!

Descem saudades
Saudades de coisa nenhuma
Saudades do Fogo,
          Amor,
Saudades da Ilha,
          Além,
Saudades de quanto não se conhece
          Saudades!

No Tarrafal,   anoitece...

                                    1966

Angola

MEMORIES AND LONGINGS

António Jacinto

From here the island of Fogo is a presence
At sunset
The palm trees are slow singers of farewell

The sail on the sea
Writes in geometry of spume
      —departure of he who remains
And the clouds carried by incessant soft breezes
      —journey of he who never left!

Come remembrances
Of nothing in particular
Of Fogo
  Love,
Of the Island
    Beyond
Remembrances of all that one does not know
    Memories and longings!

At Tarrafal, night descends...

1966

Angola

O RITMO DO TANTÃ

António Jacinto

O ritmo do tantã não tenho no sangue
nem na pele
nam na pele
tenho o ritmo do tantá no coração
no coração
no coração
o ritmo do tantã não tenho no sangue
nem na pele
nem na pele
tenho o ritmo do tantã sobretudo
mais no que pensa
mais no que pensa
Penso África, sinto África, digo África
Odeio em África
Amo em África
Estou em África
Eu também sou África
tenho o ritmo do tantã sobretudo
no que pensa
no que pensa
penso África, sinto África, digo África
E emudeço
dentro de ti, para ti África
dentro de ti, para ti África
Á fri ca
      Á fri ca
           Á fri ca

1970

Angola

THE RHYTHM OF THE TOMTOM

António Jacinto

The rhythm of the tomtom does not beat in my blood
Nor in my skin
Nor in my skin
The rhythm of the tomtom beats in my heart
In my heart
In my heart
The rhythm of the tomtom does not beat in my blood
Nor in my skin
Nor in my skin
The rhythm of the tomtom beats especially
In the way that I think
In the way that I think
I think Africa, I feel Africa, I proclaim Africa
I hate in Africa
I love in Africa
And I am Africa
The rhythm of the tomtom beats especially
In the way that I think
In the way that I think
I think Africa, I feel Africa, I proclaim Africa
And I become silent
Within you, for you, Africa
Within you, for you, Africa
A fri ca
        A fri ca
                A fri ca

1970

Angola

SAUDADIMENTO

António Jacinto

(Alda Lara)

Que marítima alga nos teus cabelos
me canta de corais e viagens além?
Que frutos nos teus olhos belos
paisagens futuras amadurecem?
Que flores estranhas do teu regaço
me juncam o caminho que faço?

Agora e aqui obriga o coração
ao aceno ausente da tua mão.

Ou luz ou verdade
esta saudade
ressuscita.

Cada dia palpita
na firmeza do aço
dum ultimo abroço!

1970

Angola

REMEMBERING

António Jacinto

To Alda Lara

What hair is this that in the wind flies
singing to me of coral and distant places?
What ripening fruit in your beautiful eyes
carries me to forgotten oases?
What flowers am I smelling on your breast?
What dream come true, what warm unrest!

Here and now my heart in these remote lands
reaches out to you and holds your absent hands.

Once again
distant friend
I see your face.

It is you that I embrace.
Vision pure and true
Today my dear I remember you!

1970

Angola

TESTAMENTO

Alda Lara

Á prostituta mais nova
do bairro mais velho e escuro
deixo os meus brincos, lavrados
em cristal, límpido e puro...

E áquela virgem esquecida,
rapariga sem ternura,
sonhando algures uma lenda,
deixo o meu vestido branco,
o meu vestido de noiva,
todo tecido de renda...

Este meu rosário antigo,
ofereço-o àquele amigo,
que não acredita em Deus...
E os livros, rosários meus
das contas de outro sofrer,
são para os homens humildes,
que nunca souberam ler.

Quanto aos meus poemas loucos,
esses, que são de dor
sincera e desordenada...
esses, que são de esperança,
desesperada mas firme,
deizo-os a ti, meu Amor...

Para que, na paz da hora,
em que a minha alma venha
beijar de longe os teus olhos,
vá por essa noite fora...
com passos feitos de luz
oferecê-los às crianças
que encontram em cada rua...

Angola

TESTAMENT

Alda Lara

To the youngest prostitute
In the oldest and darkest barrio
I leave my earrings
Cut in crystal, limpid and pure...

And to that forgotten virgin
Girl without tenderness
Dreaming somewhere of a happy story
I leave my white dress
My wedding dress
Trimmed with lace...

I offer my old rosary
To that old friend of mine
Who does not believe in God...

And my books, my rosary beads
Of a different suffering
Are for humble folk
Who never learned to read.

As for my crazy poems
Those that echo sincerely
The confusion and sadness in my heart
Those that sing of hope
Where none can be found
Those I give to you my love...

So that in a moment of peace
When my soul comes from afar
To kiss your eyes

You will go into the night
Accompanied by the moon
To read them to children
That you meet along each street...

Angola

CAMARADA COMANDANTE

Antero Abreu

Porque o amavas e te amava
O teu povo chorou-te.
Porque o amavas e te amava
Chorou-te também o nosso povo.
Camarada Comandante
Tão novo e generoso
Tão forte e ao mesmo tempor tão frágil.
Como o teu povo te chorou...
Como te chorou o nosso povo...

Da minha janela vejo
Umas hastes de buganvilia a crescer
Agarrando-se às grades à parede
A subir a subir sempre
Na ponta de uma das hastes
Uma flor carmezim abriu-se.
Ainda há pouco tempo a buganvilia foi podada...
É assim a Revolução.
Apalpando o terreno
Agarrando-se aqui e acolá
Éla cresce ela cresce...

Podem podar-lhe os ramos
Que ela cresce de novo
Inexoravelmente e com força.
Mata-se a buganvilia cortando-se-lhe a tronco.
Mas quem pode cortar o Povo?

Descansa, Camarada Comandante.
Ela cresce.

1977

Angola

CAMARADA COMANDATE

Antero Abreu

Because you love them and they loved you
Your people mourned you.
Because you loved them and they loved you
Our people also mourned you.

Comrade Comandante
So young and generous
So strong and at the same time so fragile.
How your people mourned you...
How our people mourned you...

From my window I see
Stalks of bougainvillea
Clutching the trellises on the wall
Climbing climbing always.
At the tip of one of the stalks
A crimson flower is blossoming.
Yet only a little while ago the bougainvillea was pruned...
And so it is with the Revolution.
Searching
Clutching here and there
It grows it grows...

Let them trim its branches
It grows again
Inexorably and with strength.
One kills a bougainvillea cutting its stem
But who can cut down the People?

Rest, Comrade Comandante,
It grows.

1977

Angola

POEMA SOBRE A MORTE DE AGOSTINHO NETO

Costa Andrade

Como se o dia injustamente
partisse à frente
para deizar-nos somente a noite.

Como se o mar sozinho
tivesse decidido
deixar-nos as areias moribundas.

Porque vergaste o sol, Camarada,
para levá-lo
contingo na tipóia,

não há memória, Querido Amigo,
de setembro
ter arrefecido tanto.

1979

Angola

POEM ON THE DEATH OF AGOSTINHO NETO

Costa Andrade

As if the day unjustly
departed and walked away
leaving us alone with the night.

As if the sea on its own
had withdrawn
leaving us moribund sands.

For you captured the sun, Camarada
to take with you
on your journey,

No one can remember
a September
being so cold.

1979

Angola

O CUNENE

Costa Andrade

O Cunene
não seca nem recua.
O Cunene
não seca nem se entrega
O Cunene
não seca nem se vende
O Cunene
não seca nem descansa
O Cunene
é consciencia de igualdade
O Cunene
é povo dum só povo
O Cunene
é o esforço dum por todos
O Cunene
não seca nunca mais.

1981

Angola

THE RIVER CUNENE

Costa Andrade

The Cunene
does not run dry or recede,
The Cunene
does not run dry or quit
The Cunene
does not run dry or sell itself
The Cunene
does not run dry or rest
The Cunene
is the consciousness of equality
The Cunene
is the people as one
The Cunene
is the strength of one for all
The Cunene
will never run dry.

1981

Angola

PERGUNTA

Ernesto Lara Filho

para meu Pai

Tu
Que lá em Benguela
Tinhas saudades do Minho
expressas
em todos os teus olhares saudoses
em todas as conversas

Tu
que sempre recordavas lá tão longe
a tua terra distante
o teu Portugal de Menino

Porque
Meu Pai
Me negas o direito simples
de amar a minha terra
A minha Angola
porque me negas todos os dias
a todas as horas
o direito sagrado
de ter saudades da minha terra
de olhar com os olhos embaciados
mas contentes
de escrever longas cartas inconsequentes
de ter longas conversas melancólicas
sobre a minha terra desflorada
a minha Angola adiada?

Angola

QUESTION

Ernesto Lara Filho

To my father

You who
there in Benguela
long for Minho
you show it
in all your dreamy looks
in all your conversations

You who
always would remember your far off
your distant country
the Portugal of your childhood

Why
my Father
do you deny me the simple right
to love my country
my Angola
why do you deny me each day
at all hours
the sacred right
to dream of my country
to look with eyes that do not sparkle
but are not really unhappy
to write long inconsequential letters
to carry on long melancholy conversations
about my violated country
my unfulfilled Angola?

Angola

        Serei poeta também
        adiado como a minha terra
        eu negarei Pai e Mãe
        pela minha terra
        três vezes como Pedro
        o apóstolo
        negou Cristo
        três vezes antes do galo cantar
        no raiar da madrugada.

                            1962

Angola

A poet, like my beloved country,
My dreams are yet to be realized
I will deny you Mother and Father
for my country
three times like Saint Peter
the apostle
denied Christ
three times before the cock crows
at daybreak.

1962

Angola

GUERRILHEIRO

Jofre Rocha

Conheci um guerrilheiro
pequeno mas valoroso
que enfrentou a morte
e venceu.
Era pequeno
mas nas veias carregava
obuses de raiva
e coragem
e seu sangue era rio
com o mel e o sal da vitória.

Esse querrilheiro pequeno
esse combatente sem medo
esse, és tu meu camarada.

Angola

GUERILLA FIGHTER

Jofre Rocha

I knew a guerilla fighter
small but courageous
who challenged death to combat
and won.
He was small
but in his veins
howitzers of fury
and fire
and his blood was a river
flowing with the salt and honey of victory.

That guerilla fighter
that fearless combatant
is you, my camarada.

Angola

NOVEMBRO É QUANDO

David Mestre

Novembro é quando
o silêncio ajoelha
nos homens
o beijo de duas faces
comovido

(Lágrima de
orvalho que
o cacimbo
esqueceu)

Novembro é nem
saudade
pelos braços
todos
acima

Angola

NOVEMBER IS WHEN

David Mestre

November is when
Silence kneels
Kissing
With feeling
Lovers' cheeks

Tear
Left over from
Evening dew

Nor is November
Dreaming
Of arms
beyond
reach

Angola

UM HOMEM DE CHUVA

Arlindo Barbeitos

um homem de chuva
jaz morto no chão de folhas podres

talvez só os pássaros
que parecem fazer ninho
nas ruinas das casas de nuvem
possam dar noticia

um homem de chuva
jaz morto no chão de folhas podres

Angola

A MAN OF RAIN

Arlindo Barbeitos

a man of rain
lies dead on the ground of decayed leaves

perhaps only the birds
which appear to be buiding nests
in the ruins of houses made of clouds
can notice

a man of rain
lies dead on the ground of decayed leaves

Angola

OH FLOR DA NOITE

Arlindo Barbeitos

oh flor da noite
onde todo o orvalho se perde

teus olhos
nas são estrelas
não são colibris

teus olhos
são abismos imensos
onde na escuridão
todo um passado se esconde

teus olhos
são abismos imensos
onde na escuridão
todo um futuro se forma

oh flor da noite
onde todo o orvalho se perde

teus olhos
não são estrelas
não são colibris

Angola

O NIGHT FLOWER

Arlindo Barbeitos

o night flower
where all dew is lost

your eyes
are not stars
are not hummingbirds

your eyes
are immense chasms
where in the darkness
a story from the past lies hidden

your eyes
are immense chasms
where in the darkness
a future story is germinating

o night flower
where all dew is lost

your eyes
are not stars
are not hummingbirds

Angola

A NUVEN PRODUZIU UM ELEFANTE

Arlindo Barbeitos

a nuvem produziu um elefante
o elefante pariu um coelho
das orelhas do coelho sairam montanhas
as montanhas tornaram-se tetas duma cadela prenha
das tetas da cadela prenha caiu a chuva

Angola

THE CLOUD PRODUCED AN ELEPHANT

Arlindo Barbeitos

the cloud produced an elephant
the elephant brought forth a rabbit
from the ears of the rabbit came mountains
the mountains became tits of a pregnant bitch
from the tits of the pregnant bitch rain fell

Angola

NA MATA DOS TEUS OLHOS

Arlindo Barbeitos

na mata
dos teus olhos
só se vê a noite

na noite
do leopardo
só se vê os olhos

na madrugada
da noite
só se vê os teus olhos
e
nos teus olhos
do leopardo
só se vê a mata

Angola

IN THE FOREST OF YOUR EYES

Arlindo Barbeitos

in the forest
of your eyes
only night is seen

in the night
of the leopard
only eyes are seen
in the dawn
of the night
only your eyes are seen
and
in your eyes
of the leopard
only the forest is seen

Angola

PRA O AMANHÃ

Carlos Pimentel

A Urbano Tavares Rodriques

Surgi das contradições
    craido em colonial fascismo
  não sou o homem novo

luto ser uma semente
    lançada nos camppos da Pátria
      regados pelo sangue do povo

      uma semente
        entre sementes
      do fruto do amanhã
      trazida de lugares distantes
        dentre nós todos
      coje constóiem nação

surgi das contradições
    sou vida em evolução
  com vícios não vencidos
        cheio de querer
          vencendo
     no que a forte força
        da união
      nos transforma

Não sou o homem novo
    sou sómente
        uma semente
  lançada nos campos da Pátria
        para o fruto
          colectivo
      do amanhã

1978

Angola

TOWARDS THE FUTURE

Carlos Pimentel

To Urbano Tavares Rodriques

I have emerged through contradictions
      nurtured under colonial fascism
          but I am not yet the new man

I struggle to be a seed
      sown in the fields of the Motherland
          watered by the blood of the people

One seed
    among seeds
of the fruit of the future
nurtured in distant places
    within us all
to ripen into a nation

I have emerged through contradictions
      I am life in the process of evolution
with failings not yet overcome
      Filled with desire
                triumphant
      in knowledge that the great force
        of unity
      transforms us

But I am not yet the new man
    I am only
      a single seed
sown in the fields of the Motherland
      to become the collective fruit
        of a new day.

1978

Angola

REGRESSO

João Pedro

Camarada chegou na sua terra.
(A guerra tinha acabado).
Camarada voltou na sua terra
de guerra
cansado.

Provou no gosto da boca
—sentiu salgado.
Quis falar,
abriu a boca,
—ficou calado.

Não era a terra que ele via,
quando na pausa da guerra
a descansar no capim,
sonhava com sua terra.
—Era terra assim assim.

Camarada embarcou no maximbombo,
olhou nos olhos dos homens,
viu na cara das mulheres,
tossiu no fumo do escape,
comprou bilhete e pagou.

Camarada era igual aos outros homens,
ninguém viu,
ninguém notou.

Camarada chegou na sua casa.
Bateu à porta,
esperou...
(«espera ainda camarada faz favor»).
Viu a familia,
chorou...

Angola

HOMECOMING

Joáo Pedro

Camarada arrived at his village
(the war had ended),
Camarada returned to his village
tired
from war and territory defended.

There was a taste
of salt in his mouth
as he recollected the days of violence.
He wanted to speak.
There was only silence.

This was not the village he saw
when during a lull in the war
resting on the grass
he used to dream of his village.
—It was just his village, nothing more.

Coming home in the maximbombo[1]
he looked in the eyes of the men
he looked at the faces of the women
he coughed from the exhaust
he paid for his ticket.

Camarada was just like everyone else.
no one noticed him
no one paid attention.

Camarada arrived at his house.
He knocked on the door,
and waited...
("please wait a minute camarada").
He saw his family
and he cried...

Angola

—Provou no gosto da boca,
quis falar
mas não falou.

E já lá dentro de casa
camarada adiantou:
—já cheguei na minha terra.
A guerra não acabou.

1975

Angola

—There was a taste
in his mouth
He was home from the war,
he had not died.

"I have come home"
was all that he said.
Camarada was tired
and lay down on his bed.
The war was not over.

1975

1. bus

Angola

ESPERANCA

Carlos Ferreira

E mesmo quando,
os corpos entrelaçados
as bocas se uniram,
sentimos em vagas
o tempo novo
a colher
seiva da vida.

Angola

HOPE

Carlos Ferreira

It is when
bodies intertwined
mouths united
carried on waves
we taste
the freshness
of life.

Poems from CAPE VERDE

Cape Verde

IRMÃO

Jorge Barbosa

Cruzaste Mares
na aventura da pesca da baleia,
nessas viagens para a América
de onde às vezes os navios não voltam mais.

Tens as mãos calosas de puxar
as enxárcias dos barquinhos no mar alto;
viveste horas de expectativas cruéis
na luta com as tempestades;
aboreceu-te esse tédio marítimo
das longas calmarias intermináveis.

Sob o calor infernal das fornalhas
alimentaste de carvão as caldeiras dos vapores,
    em tempo de paz
    em tempo de guerra.

E amaste com o ímpeto sensual da nossa gente
as mulheres nos países estrangeiros!

Em terra
nestas pobres Ilhas nossas
és o homem da enxada
abrindo levadas às águas das ribeiras férteis,
cavando a terra seca
nas regiões ingratas
    onde às vezes a chuva mal chega
    onde às vezes a estiagem é uma aflição
    e um cenário trágico de fome!

Levas aos teus bailes
a tua
melancolia
no fundo da tua alegria,
    quando acompanhas as Mornas com as posturas
    graves do violão
    ou apertas ao som da música crioula
    as mulheres amoráveis contra o peito...

Cape Verde

BROTHER

Jorge Barbosa

You crossed oceans and found adventure
hunting whales
and you journeyed to America
and sometimes the ships did not return.

Your hands are calloused from dragging
shrouds from the little boats on the high seas;
you lived hours of cruel expectations
in your struggle to survive storms;
you endured that maritime tedium of
long, endless days on calm seas
when you were bored to distraction.

Beneath the infernal heat of the furnace
you fed coal in the boilers of steamships
> in times of peace
> in times of war.

And with the sensual impulse of our people
you loved women from foreign lands!

On land
on these poor Islands of ours
you are the man of the hoe
clearing irrigation ditches on our fertile slopes,
digging in the dry soil
of our ungrateful earth
> where at times the necessary rains do not come
> where at times drought is a curse
> and a tragic stage for hunger!

You bring to your dancing
your melancholy
that remains in the depth of your gaiety
> when with the solemn chords of the guitar
> you accompany the singing of the Morna
> or you clasp your loving women to your breast
> to the sounds of our crioule music...

Cape Verde

A Morna...
parece que é o eco em tua alma
da voz do Mar
e da nostalgia das terras mais ao longe
que o Mar te convida,
o eco
        da voz da chuva desejada,
o eco
        da voz interior de nós todos,
        da voz da nossa tragédia sem eco!
A Morna...
tem de ti e das coisas que nos rodeiam
a expressão da nossa humildade,
a expressão passiva do nosso drama,
da nossa revolta,
        da nossa silenciosa revolta melancólica!

A América...
a América acabou-se para ti...
Fechou as portas à tua expansão!

Essas Aventuras pelos Oceanos
já não existem...
Existem apenas
nas histórias que contas do passado,
com o canhoto atravessado na boca
e risos alegres
que não chegam a esconder
        a tua
        melancolia...

O teu destino...
O teu destino
sei lá!

Viver sempre vergado sobre a terra.
a nossa terra,
        pobre
        ingrata
        querida!

Cape Verde

The Morna...
it seems that it is the echo of your soul
of the voice of the Sea
and of distant shores
that are calling you
the echo
      of your voice that cries for rain
the echo
      of the voice within us all
      of the voice of our tragedy without echo!

The Morna...
it is the expression of our lives
of our humanity
the passive expression of our drama
of our revolt
      of our silent, melancholy revolt!

America...
there is no longer the dream of America for you
America has closed its doors of immigration!
These maritime adventures
Ar no more...
They exist only
in the stories you tell of the past
as you smoke your pipe
and smile your happy smile
that cannot hide
      your melancholy...

Your destiny...
Your destiny
who knows!

To live eternally bent over the land
our poor
      ungrateful
      beloved
      land!

Cape Verde

Ser levado talvez um dia
na onda alta de alguma estiagem!
como um desses barquinhos nosses
que andam pelas Ilhas
e o Oceano acaba também por levar um dia!

Ou outro fim qualquer
humilde
anónimo...

      Ó Caboverdeano humilde
      anónimo
      —meu irmão!

1941

Cape Verde

Perhaps to be transported one day
on the high wave of another drought!
like one of our little boats
that goes from Island to Island
only to end up being carried away by the Sea!

Or perhaps another ending awaits us
quiet
anonymous...

>O gentle, anonymous
>Capeverdean
>—my brother!

1941

Cape Verde

POEMA DO MAR

Jorge Barbosa

O drama do mar,
o desassossego do Mar,
    sempre
    sempre
    dentro de nós!

O Mar!
cercando
prendendo as nossas Ilhas,
desgastando as rochas das nossas Ilhas!
Deixando o esmalte do seu salitre nas faces dos pescadores,
roncando nas areias das nossas praias,
batendo a sua voz de encontro aos montes,
baloiçando os barquinhos de pau que vão por estas costas...

O Mar!
pondo rezas nos lábios
deixando nos olhos dos que ficaram
a nostalgia resignada de países distantes
que chegam até nós nas estampas das ilustrações
nas fitas de cinema
e nesse ar de outros climas que trazem os passageiros
quando desembarcam para ver a pobreza da terra!

O Mar!
a esperança na carta de longe
que talvez não chegue mais!...

O Mar!
saudades dos velhos marinheiros contando histórias de tempos passados,
histórias da baleia que uma vez virou a canoa...
de bebedeiras, de rixes, de mulheres,
nos portos estrangeiros...

Cape Verde

POEM OF THE SEA

Jorge Barbosa

The drama of the Sea,
the turmoil of the Sea,
    always
    always
    within us!

O Sea!
encircling
embracing our Islands
wearing away the rocks of our islands!
Leaving your brine in the faces of our fishermen,
roaring upon the sands of our beaches
thundering upon our promontories
tossing our small wooden boats that go along these coasts...

O Sea!
causing prayers to come to our lips
leaving in the eyes of those who have remained
the resigned yearning for distant countries
whose images come to us in pictures
in movies
and in the ambiance of other climes brought by passengers
when they disembark to see the poverty of this land!

O Sea!
the waiting for a letter from abroad
that perhaps will come no more!...

O Sea!
memories of old men of the sea telling stories of times gone by
stories of a whale that once overturned a dory...
of drinking bouts, of fights, of women
in foreign ports...

Cape Verde

O Mar!
dentro de nós todos,
no canto da Morna,
no corpo das raparigas morenas,
nas coxas ágeis das pretas,
no desejo da viagem que fica em sonhos de muita gente!

       Este convite de toda a hora
       que o Mar nos faz para a evasão!
       Este desespero de querer partir
            e ter que ficar!

                                         1941

Cape Verde

O Sea!
within us all
in the singing of the Morna,
in the bodies of dark skinned girls,
in the supple thighs of black women,
in the longing to emigrate that remains in the dreams of many people!

> This beckoning of the Sea
> for us to escape!
> This sorrow of wanting to leave
>   but having to stay!

1941

Cape Verde

REGRESSO

Jorge Barbosa

Navio aonde vais
deitado sobre o mar?

Aonde vais
levado pelo vento?

Que rumo é o teu
navio do mar largo?

Aquele país talvez
onde a vida
é uma grande promessa
e um grande deslumbramento!

Leva-me contigo
navio.

Mas torna-me a trazer!

1956

Cape Verde

RETURN

Jorge Barbosa

Ship where are you going
lying on the sea?

Where are you going
carried by the wind?

What course is yours
ship of the broad sea?

That country perhaps
where life
is a great promise
and a great fascination!

Take me with you
ship.

But bring me back!

1956

Cape Verde

BOA VIAGEM

Jorge Barbosa

Para Gabriel Mariano

Vai amigo!
Pressinto
já longe
a tua figura
timida cruzando
meridianos invisíveis
na distância do tempo.

Vai amigo!
an supersónica
vertigem do voo
    por entre
      muvens e céus
na disparada louca
dos pneus
macios a rolarem
em estradas de asfalto.

Vejo-te
amigo
assim
neste tau jeito
quase triste
passeando no deck
os passos
lentos
medidos
a cabeleira
lírica
desfeita
pelo sopro salgado da brisa.

Cape Verde

BON VOYAGE

Jorge Barbosa

For Gabriel Mariano

Go friend!
I have an image
far from here
of your timid face
as you cross
invisible meridians
in the distance of time.

Go friend!
on that jet
dizziness of flight
    between
    clouds and sky
with the fiery screeching
of smooth tires
racing down an asphalt runway.

I see you
friend
now
in your almost sad
manner
strolling on deck
your steps
slow
measured
your hair
lyrically
blowing
in the salty breezes
of the sea.

Cape Verde

        O paquete
        marchando solene
        deixando
        longo
        traço fosforescente
        a cintilar
        nos rumos do mar.

Subirás
brancas montanhas
de gelo e de neve.
    Do alto verás
    panoramas e cores
    como não há
    nas nossas ilhas.

    Vai amigo!
Vejo-te assim
sonolento e fatigado
cavalgando
o dorso de um camelo
em vagarosa
marcha por desertos
intérminos ao sol.
    O vento depois apagará
    a passagem da caravana
    marcada nas areias.

Este tau ar triunfal!
o capacete o calção
a espingarda
de caçador
o pé direito
firmado sobre a juba
de um leão abatido!

    Via amigo!
vejo-te passar
por exóticos
portos
de ilhas distantes.
    Alguma mulher
    talvez
    num cais acenando...

Cape Verde

Steamer
advancing solemnly
leaving in its wake
a long phosphorescent
trail

You will climb
mountains white
with snow and ice.
>   From the summit you will see
>   colors and panoramas
>   that don't exist
>   on our islands.

>   Go friend!

I see you now
weary and tired
riding on
the back of a camel
on a slow
journey over an endless desert
under an unforgiving sun.
>   Your caravan will get lost
>   as sandstorms blind you
>   taking you from
>   your desired route.

Here you are with your air of victory
a pith helmet, breeches
a hunter's
rifle
your right foot
firmly placed on the mane
of a fallen lion!

>   Go friend!

I see you passing
through exotic
ports
on distant islands.
>   A woman
>   perhaps
>   on a wharf...beckoning...

Cape Verde

      Vai amigo!
      vai
      agora que és jovem.

E conta
   as paisagens
   as maravilhas
   os amores...
Manda fotografias
   de Paris
   do Congo
   de Nanquim
   da esátua da Liberdade
   das Pirâmides
   do Danúbio
   da Grande Muralha.

Se passares a Cortina
Cuidado amigo!
Cuidado amigo!
Manda fotografias do Kremlin.

Manda uma também
do Imperador do Japão
vestido à americana.

     O mundo é grande!

   Vai
agora que é cedo
agora que és jovem
agora que és poeta
e tens fé
nas tuas ilusões.

   Amigo!
o mundo é grande!
A nossa terra é que é
pequena e melancólica
perdida no mar

Cape Verde

    Go friend!
    go
    while you are young.

And tell about
    landscapes
    life's wonders
    lovers

Send pictures of
    Paris
    the Congo
    Nanking
    the Statue of liberty
    the Pyramids
    the Danube
    the Great Wall

If you pass through the Iron Curtain
Be careful friend!
Be careful friend!
Send pictures from the Kremlin.

Send one too
of the Emperor of Japan
dressed in American style.

    The world is great!

    Go
while there is time
while you are young
while you are a poet
and have faith
in your illusions.

    Friend!

the world is great!
And our bit of land is
so small so sad
lost in the middle of the ocean.

Cape Verde

> (Agora
> aqui me confesso
> no fim deste poema
> o jovem amigo
> o poeta
> a quem me refiro
>   não há...
> O que há é um lirico
> sexagenário
> aqui disfarçado...)
>
> Boa Viagem!
> Boa Viagem!

Cape Verde

(Now
let me confess
at the end of this poem
the young friend
the poet
to whom I am referring
There is no...
what there is is a
lyrical sexagenarian
playing a role...)

Bon Voyage!
Bon Voyage!

Cape Verde

CRIOULO

Manuel Lopes

Há em ti a chama que arde com inquietação
e o lume íntimo, escondido, dos rescaldos
—que é o calor que tem mais duração.
A terra onde nasceste deu-te a coragem e a resignação.
Deu-te a fome nas estiagens dolorosas.
Deu-te a dor para que nela
sofrendo, fosses mais humano.
Deu-te a provar da sua taça o agricdoce da compreensão,
e a humildade que nasce do desengano...

E deu-te esta esperança desenganada
em cada um dos dias que virão
e esta alegria guardada
para a manhã esperada
em vão...

Cape Verde

CRIOULE

Manuel Lopes

Within you burns a restless fire
Its eternal flame hidden in the embers
—it is a warmth that endures.
The land where you were born gave you courage and resignation.
It gave you hunger in times of sorrowful droughts
It gave you suffering
To make you more human.
It gave you the bittersweet taste of the cup of understanding
And the humility which is born of deception and pain...
And it gave you this pure faith
In each upcoming day
And this happiness kept
For mornings we wait for
In vain...

Cape Verde

CAIS

Manual Lopes

Nunca parti deste cais
e tenho o mundo na mão!
Para mim nunca é demais
responder sim
cinquenta vezes a cada não.

Por cada barco que me negou
cinquenta partem por mim
e o mar é plano e o céu azul sempre que vou!

Mundo pequeno para quem ficou...

1943

Cape Verde

QUAY

Manuel Lopes

Not once did I depart from this quay[1]
yet I have the world in my hand!
It is always easy for me
fifty times to answer yes
for each no that holds me to this land.

For each boat that leaves without me I feel pain
I sail on fifty others and am blessed
and the sky is blue and the sea at rest!

Small world for he who must remain...

1943

1. There are several published versions of this poem. This is the original version and is the one preferred by Manuel Lopes. Written in 1943, it was published in his book Crioulo e Outros Poemas (1964).

Cape Verde

POEMA DO RAPAZ TORPEDEADO

Osvaldo Alcântara

Éramos vinte numa jangada,
e o rapaz torpedeado connosco.
Havia trinta dias
que andávamos à tona de água
e já não tínhamos comida,
e já não tínhamos mais água.

E o rapaz torpedeado contou a sua história.

> «Uma vez um rapaz moço morreu
> porque queria ver o mundo.
> Mas o mundo queria
> era sentir-se orgulhoso do seu poder.
> E o rapaz moço morreu
> porque queria ver o mundo.»

Tínhamos tido latas de alimento sintético
e de leite condensado,
fomos adiante vivendo
da história do rapaz torpedeado.

Cape Verde

POEM OF THE BOY WHO HAD BEEN TORPEDOED

Osvaldo Alcântara

There were twenty of us on the raft
including the lad who had been torpedoed.
For thirty days
we floated aimlessly
we had run out of food
and we had run out of water.

And the torpedoed lad told his story.

> "Once a young boy died
> because he wanted to see the world.
> But the proud world felt
> a need to show off its power.
> And the young boy died
> because he wanted to see the world."

We had tins of synthetic food
and condensed milk,
We continued on living off
the story of the lad who had been torpedoed.

FAMINTO

Oswaldo Alcântara

Ele chegou à minha porta;
os seus olhos não tinham brilho,
bem certo que eles não poderiam mais colaborar na maravilha da vida.
As suas mãos já não tinham aquele jeito potente de quem vai criar.
Ele não vinha para me matar,
trazia apenas o modo pedinte de quem quer viver mais um dia,
mas tive medo da palavra que sairia da sua boca.
Ele vinha nu, dei-lhe os restos de uma manta velha
para se cobrir do frio.
Dei roupa para o seu corpo,
dei pão para a sua fome.
Fui seu irmão e tive pejo de lhe confessar
que a mesma penumbra contornava
as nossas duas sombras fatigadas
desta caminhada sem itinerário.
Eu devia ter clamado, para todos ouvirem, que ele era o desterrado,
e ensinar-lhe o caminho para ele se libertar da sua renuncia.
Nada disso.
O que fiz foi somente dar-lhe a moeda das grandes traições.
No meu sangue ficou para sempre o travo desta culpa.

Cape Verde

VICTIM OF FAMINE

Osvaldo Alcântara

He came to my door;
there was no light in his eyes.
Surely they would not be able to express the wonder of life.
His hands had lost that vital strength of one who lives and works.
He had not come to kill me,
he came with the resigned expression of one who just hoped to survive
                                                      one more day,
but was afraid of the words he would utter.
He was naked, I provided him with an old tattered blanket
to protect himself from the cold.
I gave him clothing for his body
and bread for his hunger.
I was his brother and to my shame I acknowledged to him
that we are all tired shadows
traveling the same unsure road
bathed in the same obscure light.
I should have cried out for all to hear that he and not I had been
                                                      exiled from life's feast
and I should have shown him a way to avoid giving up.
None of this.
All I did was offer coins of betrayal.
The bitterness of my guilt will not go away.

Cape Verde

BARCOS

Yolanda Morazzo

*A querida ilha de São Vicente
de Cabo Verde.*

«Nha terra ê quel piquinino
e São Vicente ê quê di meu.»

Nas praias
Da minha infância
Morrem barcos
Desmantelados.

Fantasmas
De pescadores
Contrabandistas

Desaparecidos
Em qualquer vaga
Nem eu sei onde.

E eu sou a mesma
Tenho dez anos
Brinco na areia
Empunho os remos...
Canto e sorrio
A embaracação:
Para o mar!
É para o mar!...

E o pobre barco
O barco triste
Cansado e frio
Não se moveu...

1962

Cape Verde

BOATS

Yolanda Morazzo

*For my beloved island of
São Vicente in Cape Verde*

On the beaches
Of my childhood
Dead, dismantled
Boats

Ghosts
Of fishermen
Of smugglers
Lost
At sea
I don't know where.

I am the same little girl
I am ten years old
I am playing in the sand
I am holding the oars
I am singing and smiling
At the boat
About to begin its journey:
To the sea!
To the sea!

But the poor boat
The sad boat
Tired and cold
Did not move...

1962

Cape Verde

CARTA DE LONGE

Gabriel Mariano

Para Orlando Levy

Carta de longe lembrando
a dispersão dolorosa.
Carta de Boston América
de Jorge Pedro Barbosa.

Eram quarenta e só quatro
em Caboverde ficaram.

Tinha Brasil Argentina
tinha Dakar-Senegal.
América vinha primeiro
já nos obscuros caminhos.

Já nos obscuros caminhos
da encruzilhada inicial
já insinuando por perto
Brasil Dakar-Senegal.

Tinha Guiné Moçambique
Angola veio e depos
Macau Timor Venezuela
Goa Brasil São-Tomé
e dos quarenta só quatro
em Caboverde ficaram.

Caminhos brandos pra quem
os pés já sangram doridos
ainda meninos os pés
os pés já sangram doridos.

Ó meus destinos inquietos
no inquieto mapa do mundo.
Eram quarenta e só quatro
em Caboverde ficaram.

1965

Cape Verde

LETTER FROM ABROAD

Gabriel Mariano

For Orlando Levy

A letter from abroad brings to mind again
our sad diaspora.
A letter from Jorge Pedro Barbosa my friend
from Boston America

We were forty and four
stayed in Cape Verde.

There was Brazil, Argentina
Dakar-Senegal.
But America ranked first
of the places of our exile.

We heard the beckoning call
of geographically closer ports
Some were off to Dakar-Senegal
others to Brazil.

There was Guiné Mozambique
then came Angola and after that
Macau Timor Venezuela
Goa Brazil São Tomé
and of our group of forty only four
stayed in Cape Verde.

I remember happy adventures of our childhood.
Even as kids our bloody feet ached.
Years have passed and we still ache.
Our feet still ache.

Oh my restless friends who followed
their destiny to the restless corners of the world.
We were forty and only four
stayed in Cape Verde.

1965

Cape Verde

ANTI-EVASÃO

Ovídio Martins

*Ao camarada poeta
João Vário*

Pedirei
Suplicarei
Chorarei

    Não vou para Pasárgada

Atirar-me-ei ao chão
e prenderei nas mãos convulsas
ervas e pedras de sangue

    Não vou para Pasárgada

Gritarei
Berrarei
Matarei

    Não vou para Pasárgada

1962

Cape Verde

ANTI-EVASION

Ovídio Martins

*To Camarada poet
João Vário*

I will beg
I will plead
I will cry
      I will not go to Pasárgada

I will throw myself on the ground
and with bleeding hands
I will not let go
of grass or stone
      I will not go to Pasárgada

I will scream
I will shout
I will kill
      I will not go to Pasárgada

1962

Cape Verde

LEMA

Onésimo Silveira

Atrás dos ferros da prisão
É preciso levantar os braços algemados
Contra a prepotência!

Atrás dos ferros da prisão
É preciso afogar a noite em gritos de luz
Para a voz de todos os homens!

Atrás dos ferros da prisão
É precisco lutar pelo pão das crianças sem pão:
As criancas de barriga inchada
De lombriga e de fome!

1962

Cape Verde

LEMMA

Onésimo Silveira

Behind prison bars
It is necessary to raise our shackled hands
Against oppression!

Behind prison bars
It is necessary to suffocate the night with shouts of light
For the voice of all mankind!

Behind prison bars
It is necessary to struggle for children without bread:
Children with stomachs swollen
From roundworm and starvation!

1962

MINDELO

Corsino Fortes

Entre a escuridão
E o silêncio da noite...
Amachucado

Entre a morna e o violão
Sonho... Mindelo
De mãos apoiadas
Sobre o eco da tua pulsação.

Mindelo
Recanto de sonhadores
De poetas e músicos
De aves sem asas
Voando
Em busca de alvo
Na neblina da noite.

Orvalho de lágrima
Gota de saudade
Alegria escurecida
Pelo negrume da vida.

Mindelo
Tuas pedras são sonhos
Tuas brisas ilusões
Tuas ruas são rios
Por onde deslizam lágrimas
Envoltas em sorrisos.

MINDELO

Corsino Fortes

Amidst the darkness
And the silence of night...
I am weary

Amidst the sad sounds of the morna and the guitar
I dream... Mindelo
My hands feeling
The echo of your pulse.

Mindelo
Quiet retreat of dreamers
And poets and musicians
Of wingless birds
Flying
Searching
In the mist of the night.

Teardrop
The dew of dreams
Happiness obscured
By night's blackness.

Mindelo
Your stones are dreams
Your breezes illusions
Your streets are rivers
Where tears flow
Wrapped in smiles.

Cape Verde

Mindelo
Ó doce Mindelo morno
De lua nascente e poente
De noite debruçado
Na morna dolente
De poesia encostada
Na esquina da noite.

Mindelo de Luzes
de Pétalas e Prantos
O quimera perdida
O berço adormecido
    embalado
Dentro de mim!

1959

Cape Verde

Mindelo
O sweet Mindelo softened with
The light of the rising and setting moon
The night bent over listening
To the sorrowful sounds of the morna
Poetry leaning against
The corner of the night.

Mindelo of light
Of Petals and Tears
O lost chimera
O cradle sleeping
      rocking
Within me!

1959

Cape Verde

LISBOA - 1971

Arménio Vieira

*A Ovídio Martins
e Osvaldo Osório*

Em verdade Lisboa não estava ali para nos saudar.

Ei-nos enfim transidos e quase perdidos
no meio de guardas e aviões da Portela.

Em verdade éramos o gado mais pobre
d'África trazido àquele lugar
e como folhas varridas pela vassoura do vento
nossos paramentos de presunção e de casta.

E quando mais tarde surpreendemos o espanto
da mulher que vendia maçãs
e queria saber d'onde...ao que vínhamos
descobrimos o logro a circular no coração do Império.

Porém o desencanto, que desce ao peito
e trepa a montanha,
necessita da levedura que a tempo fornece.

E num camião, por entre caixotes e resquicios da véspera,
fomos seguindo nosso destino
naquela manhã friorenta e molhada por chuviscos d'inverno.

Cape Verde

LISBON - 1971

Arménio Vieira

*To Ovídio Martins
and Osvaldo Osório*

In truth Lisbon was not there to welcome us.

Here we were shivering and all but lost
amidst the guards and planes of Portela.

In truth we were the most miserable
of Africa's cattle brought to that place
and like leaves swept by brooms of wind
our chasubles of presumptions and race.

And later when we were startled
by the shocked expression of the woman selling apples
who wanted to know from where...and why...we had come
we discovered disillusion circulating in the heart of the Capital.

However disenchantment which descends to the pit of the stomach
and climbs mountains
needs time to be fermented.

And in a truck between crates and residue from the day before
we were following our destiny
on that morning made cold and wet by winter's rains.

Cape Verde

SINOPSE PARA UM REGRESSO À INFÂNCIA

João Rodrigues

Quando a chuva vier
Hei-de voltar aos tempos de criança!

(Nu
E descalço
O menino doutrora
Voltará a banhar-se nas águas da chuva
Caindo
Doce e mansa
Mansa e fria
Pelos beirais dos casebres da sua aldeia...)

Hei-de medir as peugadas antigas
Dos pegueninos pés
—Ainda as descobrirei
Na terra-vermelha-molhada
Das ribeiras da minha aldeia!—
Para que saiba fazer as contas
Dos anos que passaram...

Hei-de vingar o tempo
Que me roubou a infância!

Verei na água-vermelha-das-ribeiras
O sangue da minha vinganca
E no seu sussurro pro mar correndo
Ouvirei um gemido de dor
—Punhal cravando-se no coração
Da terra-vermelha-ensopada.

Vingarei o tempo
Que me roubou a infância!

Cape Verde

SYNOPSIS FOR A RETURN TO CHILDHOOD

João Rodrigues

It is when the rains come
That I return to the days of my childhood![1]

(Naked
And barefoot
I am the child of another time
Returning to bathe in the rainwater
Dripping
Slowly, gently
Off the eaves of the huts in my village...)

I examine the old tracks
Made by tiny feet
—again I discover them for the first time
In the wet red earth
Along the arroyos of my village!—
So that now I can write stories
Of those years that have disappeared...

I seek to recapture time
Stolen from me by my childhood!

I see again in waters turned red running over the red earth
The blood of my own revenge
And in its murmurings as it races to the sea
I hear sad moanings
—a dagger burying itself in the heart
Of the wet red earth.

I seek to recapture time
Stolen from me by my childhood!

Cape Verde

Depois
Beijarei a chuva
Caindo
Doce e mansa
Mansa e fria
Sobre os casebres da minha aldeia...

Nu
E descalço
Caminharei sobre a lama-vermelha-das-ribeiras
(Serei o menino doutroro)
     —Como há tantos anos!

Afterwards
I shall kiss the rain
Falling
Slowly, gently
On the huts of my village...
Naked
And barefoot
Once again I am walking on the red mud of the arroyos
(I am once again a child)
    —As I was so many years ago!

1. This poem was originally published at the beginning of João Rodrigues' autobiographical novel of his childhood <u>Cases e Casinhotos</u> (<u>Houses and Hovels</u>).

Cape Verde

A ILHA E A EUROPA

Luís Silva

Ao Luíz Romano

Da Ilha à Europa
Caminhamos sonhando a liberdade
E dinheiro para a cachupa da familia.

A liberdade, bem me lembro dizíamos
Estava para além dos Pirinéus
E que o dinheiro para cachupa, esse agora,
Andava sobre o mar
E como caboverdianos, marinheiros de sempre,
Iríamos conquistá-lo com o fruto do nosso suor.

O mais cedo voltaríamos para a solução final;
—Desafiar funcionários, polícias,
Toda a escória que suga a Terra-Mãe.

Cape Verde

THE ISLAND AND EUROPE

Luís Silva

To Luíz Romano

From the Island to Europe
We have journeyed chasing dreams of freedom
And money to buy cachupa to feed our families.

Freedom, I well remember, we used to say
Lay beyond the Pyrenees
And money for cachupa, that
Was found over the sea.

And we Capeverdeans, eternal seafarers.
Would conquer our dreams with the fruit of our labor.

We planned on returning as soon as possible for our final task;
—To confront government clerks, the police,
That entire mob that suck dry our Motherland.

Cape Verde

O FILHO DO EMIGRANTE

Luís Silva

Aquela crianca franzina
Que se esquiva à neve e à chuva
Blusão preto
Corpo Serrado
Boína entola na cabeca
E mãos nos bolços
É um imigrante.

Fala francês
Conhece bem a história de Napoleão
Leu Sartre e Teillard de Chardin.

Contudo, gostaria de saber um pouco da sua Terra...
Diáriamente é confrontado à segregação racial dos colegas,
E se interroga sobre as causas da sua presença nesta TERRA!
Os pais, fatigados pela dura faina quotidiana
Desviam as suas perguntas com um simples olhar de tristeza.
Querem regressar de férias no proximo ano
E assim são obrigados a trabalhar 16 horas diãrias.

Se Deus quiser irá também!
Que o seu corpo franzino
         supporte
            Invernos
               Racismo
               e outras misérias!...

Cape Verde

THE EMIGRANT'S SON

Luís Silva

That thin little boy
Bundled up to protect himself
From the rain and the snow
Black smock
Frail body
Moth eaten beret pulled down over his head
And hands in his pockets—
He's an immigrant.

He speaks French
He knows the history of Napoleon
He has read Sartre and Teilhard de Chardin.

Nevertheless, he would like to know something of his
Country...
Each day he must face the racism of his schoolmates,
And ask himself why he must live in this Country!
His parents, exhausted from hard daily struggle
Deflect his questions with a simple look of sadness.
They hope to return home next year on holiday
And to do so they must work sixteen hours a day.

If God wills, he'll go too!
If only his thin little body
        Can survive
           Winter
              Racism
                    and other miseries!...

EMIGRANTE

Ana Júlia

O drama começa no momento
em que nasce a ideia de "partir"
Aí param os sonhos
E começam os pesadelos.

Emigrante!

Esta é a alcunha que te deram.

A tragédia que isso acarreta
consome anos de existência
aniquilando lentamente
castelos edificados de ilusões
que dos sonhos ainda restam.

Emigrante!

Fantasia dos que ficam

Américas
Alemanhas
Franças
e outros mundos sempre iguais...

Emigrante!

Suportar esse título tão honradamente
ter que comer o pão que o diabo amassou
ser sempre forasteiro em porta alheia...

Sim, emigrante!

Cape Verde

EMIGRANT

Ana Júlia

The drama begins the moment
the idea is born "to leave"
At that instant dreams end
and nightmares begin.

Emigrant!

That is what you are known as.

The side effects of this tragedy
consume years of existence
slowly destroying
castles nurtured on illusions
that still remain as dreams.

Emigrant!

Fantasies of those who remain, images of

America
Germany
France
and other worlds always the same...

Emigrant!

To bear this name with dignity
to have to eat bread kneaded by the devil
to be always an outsider in a distant port...

Yes, emigrant!

Cape Verde

Emigrante: sobrevivência
Gritos de alma
ambição amordaçada
desejos frustados...

VITA BREVIS num copo de vinho
Esquecer as amarguras
"Da Terra Prometida"

Cape Verde

Emigrant: overcoming
cries of the soul
ambition stymied
desires frustrated...

VITA BREVIS in a glass of wine
in order to forget the pains of
"The Promised Land."

Poems from GUINÉ BISSAU

Guiné Bissau

NAUS SEM RUMO

Amílcar Cabral

Dispersas,
emersas,
sòzinhas sôbre o Oceano...
Sequiosas,
rochosas,
pedaços do Africano
do negro continente
as engeitadas filhas,
nossas ilhas,
navegam tristemente...

Qual naus da antiguidade,
qual naus
do velho Portugal,
aquelas que as entradas
do imenso mar abriram...
As naus
que as nossas descobriram.

Ao vento, à tempestade,
navegam
de Cabo Verde as ilhas,
as filhas
do ingente
e negro continente...

São dez as caravelas
em busca do Infinito...
São dez as caravelas,
sem velas,
embusca do Infinito...
À tempestade e ao vento,
caminham...
navegam mansamente
as ilhas,
as filhas
do negro continente...

Guiné Bissau

SHIPS WITHOUT MOORINGS

Amílcar Cabral

Dispersed
emersed
alone on the Ocean...
thirsty
rocky
bits of Africa
the dark continent
rejected daughters
our islands
navigate in sadness...

What ships of antiquity
what ships
from old Portugal,
those that set sail
on the immense seas...
Ships
that discovered our ships.

In wind, in storm
they navigated
the islands of Cape Verde
daughters
of the enormous
black continent...

They are ten the caravels
searching for the infinite...
They are ten the caravels
without sails
searching for the infinite...
In storm and in wind
they travel...
gently they navigate
these islands
these daughters
of the black continent.

Guiné Bissau

—Onde ides naus da Fome,
da Morna,
do Sonho,
e da Desgraça?...

—Onde ides?...

Sem rumo e sem ter fito,
sòzinhas,
dispersas,
emersas,
nós vamos,
sonhando,
sofrendo,
em busca do Infinito!...

Guiné Bissau

Where are you going ships of Hunger
of the Morna
of Dreams
and of Calamity?
Where are you going?

Adrift without destination
alone,
dispersed,
emersed,
we go on,
dreaming,
suffering,
in search of the infinite!

Guiné Bissau

O SILÊNCIO

Carlos d'Almada

Um poeta morreu
               Lutando
contra o retrocesso
             vergonhoso

Nas suas veias, pouco a pouco
o sangue
           coagula-se
               como pedra

De repente
       um sorriso leve
aparece nos seus labios
e nos olhos ardentes
             surge
uma estrela negra que canta:
«Cabral devia viver, porque
ele e a alma deste navio»

                                  1980

Guiné Bissau

SILENCE

Carlos d'Almada

A poet died
    Fighting
against shameful
retrogression

In his veins, little by little
blood
    coagulates
        like stone

Suddenly
    a slight smile
appears on his lips
and in his glowing eyes
    appears
a black star that sings:
"Cabral must be alive, because
he is the soul of this ship"

1980

Poems from MOZAMBIQUE

Mozambique

DEIXA PASSAR O MEU POVO

Noémia de Sousa

Noite morna de Moçambique
e sons longínquos de marimba chegam até mim
—certos e constantes—
vindos nem eu sei donde.
Em minha casa de madeira e zinco,
abro o rádio e deixo-me embalar...
Mas as vozes da América remexem-me a alma e os nervos.
E Robeson e Marian cantam para mim
spirituals negros de Harlem.
«Let my people go»
—oh deixa passar o meu povo,
deixa passar o meu povo—,
dizem.
E eu abro os olhos e já não posso dormir.
Dentro de mim soam-me Anderson e Paul
e não são doces vozes de embalo.
«Let my people go».

Nervosamente,
sento-me à mesa e escrevo...
(Dentro de mim,
deixa passar o meu povo,
«oh let my people go...»)
E já não sou mais que instrumento
do meu sangue em turbilhão
com Marian me ajudando
com sua voz profunda - minha Irmã.

Escrevo...
Na minha mesa, vultos familiares se vêm debruçar.
Minha Mãe de mãos rudes e rosto cansado
e revoltas, dores, humilhações,
tatuando de negro o virgem papel branco.
E Paulo, que não conheço

Mozambique

LET MY PEOPLE GO

Noémia de Sousa

Warm night in Mozambique
and distant sounds of the marimba come to me
—sure and constant
coming from I don't know where.
In my house of wood and zinc
I turn on the radio and begin to doze off...
But voices from America stir my soul and my senses.
Robeson and Marion are singing for me
negro spirituals from Harlem
"Let my people go"—
they sing
And I open my eyes and I can sleep no more.
Anderson and Paul are ringing in my soul
and theirs are not sweet soothing voices to lull one to sleep
"Let my people go."

Nervously
I sit down at my table and I write...
(Within me
"oh let my people go...")
And I am but the instrument
of my excited blood
with Marion with her deep voice
inspiring me — my Sister.

I am writing...
At my desk familiar images peer at me.
My Mother with her rough hands and tired face
and revolts, sufferings, humiliations
tattooing in black the virgin white paper.
And Paulo, whom I do not know

Mozambique

mas é do mesmo sangue da mesma seiva amada de Moçambique,
e misérias, janelas gradeadas, adeuses de magaíças,
algodoais, e meu inesquecível companheiro branco
e Zé — meu irmão — e Saul,
e tu, Amigo de doce olhar azul,
pegando na minha mão e me obrigando a escrever
com o fel que me vem da revolta.
Todos se vêm debruçar sobre o meu ombro,
enquanto escrevo, noite adiante,
com Marian e Robeson vigiando pelo olho luminoso do rádio
—«let my people go».
oh let my people go.

E enquanto me vierem de Harlem
vozes de lamentação
e os meus vultos familiares me visitarem
em longas noites de insónia,
não poderei deixar-me embalar pela música fútil
das valsas de Strauss.
Escreverei, escreverei,
com Robeson e Marian gritando comigo:
«Let my people go»
OH DEIXA PASSAR O MEU POVO.

1953

Mozambique

but we share the same blood and the same beloved fibre of Mozambique
and miseries, prison windows and good byes
of contract laborers off to the mines in South Africa,
cotton plantations and my unforgetable white companion,
and Zé — my brother — and Saul
and you, Friend with sweetness in your blue eyes,
holding my hand, obliging me to write
from the gall that fills me when I cry out in protest.
All these images come to me, stooping over my shoulder
while I am writing, as the night progresses,
with Marion and Robeson watching me
—"let my people go.
oh let my people go."

And while these voices of lamentation
come to me from Harlem
and while my familiar images visit me
during long nights of insomnia,
I will not let myself be lulled to sleep by the futile music
of Strauss waltzes.
I will write, I will write
with Robeson and Marion shouting with me:
"Let my people go"
OH LET MY PEOPLE GO.

1953

Mozambique

ONDE ESTOU

Kalungano

Não

Não me procureis
onde não existo

Eu vivo
curvado sobre a terra
seguindo o caminho inscrito
pelo chicote
nas minhas costas nuas

Eu vivo
nos portos
alimentando as fornalhas
movendo as máquinas
pelo caminho dos homens

Eu vivo
no corpo de minha mãe
vendendo a minha carne
o meu sexo
não é para amar

Eu vivo
perdido nas ruas
de uma civilzação
que me esmaga
com ódio
sem pena

E se é a minha voz que se ouve
e se sou eu que canto ainda
é porque não posso morrer
Mas só a lua escuta a minha dor

Mozambique

WHERE I AM

Kalungano

No

Do not
look for me
where I do not exist

I live
bent over the earth
following the path proscribed
by the whip
lacerating my black back

I live
in the ports
stoking furnaces
moving machines
for man's progress

I live
in the body of my mother
selling my flesh
my sex
is not for love

I live
lost in the streets
of a civilization
that crushes me
with hatred
without pity

And if my voice is heard
and if I continue to sing
it is because I cannot die
But only the moon listens to my grief

Mozambique

Não

não me procureis

nos grandes salões
onde não estou
onde não posso estar

Aqui na América

Sim
eu estou também
eu estou

Mas Lincoln
foi assassinado
e eu
       eu
             eu
todos os dias soul linchado

O comboio especial
rolando vertiginosamente na estrada
é ouro
é sangue
que eu verti através dos séculos

Porquê
pois
procurar-me na Glória de Beethoven

se eu estou aqui

erguendo-me
nos milhões de ais
que se elevam dos porões
em todos os cais

Mozambique

No

Do not
look for me
in the grand salons
where I am not to be found
where I am not allowed

Here in America

Yes I am here as well
I am here

But Lincoln
was assassinated
and I
I
I
I am lynched every day

The special train
vertiginously rolling on its journey
it is gold
it is my blood
spilled over the centuries

Why
then
look for me in the Gloria of Beethoven

if I am here
lifting myself up
in the million cries of protest
emanating in the holds
in all the docks

Mozambique

se eu estou aqui
bem vivo
na voz de Robeson e Hughes
Césaire e Guillén

Godido e Black Boy renascidos

nas entranhas da terra
transformando com o meu corpo
os alicerces da vida

se eu estou aqui

soma consciente e firme
dos homens
que compuseram o poema

da vida contra a morte

do fim da noite
e do começo do dia.

1958

Mozambique

if I am here
very much alive
in the voice of Robeson and Hughes
Césaire and Guillén

Godido and Black Boy reborn

in the bowels of the earth
transforming with my body
the foundations of life

if I am here
firm and conscious sum
of those men
who composed the poem

of life against death
of night's end
and day's beginning

1958

Mozambique

GRITO NEGRO

José Craveirinha

Eu sou carvão!
E tu arrancas-me brutalmente do chão
E fazes-me tua mina
Patrão!

Eu sou carvão!
E tu acendes-me, patrão
Para te servir eternamente como força motriz
mas eternamente não
Patrão!

Eu sou carvão!
E tenho que arder, sim
E queimar tudo com a força da minha combustão.

Eu sou carvão!
Tenho que arder na exploração
Arder até às cinzas da maldição
Arder vivo como alcatrão, meu Irmão
Até não ser mais tua mina
Patrão!

Eu sou carvão!
Tenho que arder
E queimar tudo com o fogo da minha combustão.

Sim!
Eu serei o teu carvão
Patrão!

Mozambique

BLACK PROTEST

José Craveirinha

I am coal!
And you uproot me brutally from the earth
And make me your mine
Boss!

I am coal!
And you set me on fire, boss
To serve you eternally as a source of energy
But not eternally
Boss!

I am coal!
And yes, it is my nature to become heat
And burn everything with the force of my combustion.

I am coal!
I must burn your world of exploitation
Burn until I become cinders of malediction
Burn with live heat like tar, my Brother
Until I am no longer your mine
Boss!

I am coal!
It is my nature to become heat
And burn everything with the fire from my combustion.

Yes!
I will be your coal
Boss!

Mozambique

CANTIGA DO BATELÃO

José Craveirinha

Se me visses morrer
os milhões de vezes que nasci

Se me visses chorar
os milhões de vezes que te riste...

Se me visses gritar
os milhões de vezes que me calei...

Se me visses cantar
os milhões de vezes que morri
e sangrei..

Digo-te irmão europeu
havias de nascer
havias de chorar
havias de cantar
havias de gritar

E havias de sofrer
a sangrar vivo
milhões de mortes como Eu!!!

Mozambique

SONG OF THE GREAT BARGE

José Craveirinha

If you saw me dying
the millions of times I was being born

If you saw me crying
the millions of times that you were laughing...

If you saw me shouting
the millions of times I was silent...

If you saw me singing
the millions of times I was dying
and bleeding...

I say to you European brother
you will be born
you will cry
you will sing
you will shout

And you will suffer
bleed bleed
millions of deaths like Me!!

Mozambique

UM HOMEM NUNCA CHORA

José Craveirinha

Acreditava naquela história
do homem que nunca chora.

Eu julgave-me um homem.

Na adolescência
meus filmes de aventuras
punham-me muito longe de ser cobarde
na arrogante criancice do herói de ferro.

Agora tremo.
E agora choro.

Como um homem treme.
como chora um homem!

Mozambique

A MAN NEVER CRIES

José Craveirinha

I used to believe that story
that a man never cries.

And I used to think I was a man.

In my youth
I dared not be a coward
when we played our arrogant games of childhood
imitating the heroic man of steel in the movies.

Now I tremble
And now I cry.

As a man trembles.
As a man cries!

Mozambique

CELA 1

José Craveirinha

Aqui estou neurasténico
como um cão
danado a lamber a salgada
crosta das velhas feridas.

Em que língua
e com que rosto
aos meus filhos órfãos de pai
eu vou dizer que se esqueçam?

Mozambique

CELL 1

José Craveirinha

Here I am neurasthenic
like a dog
gone mad licking salty
scabs of old wounds.

With what words
and with what face
am I going to tell
my orphaned children to forget their father?

Mozambique

MULATO

Rui Knopfli

Sou branco, escolhi-te.
Hoje durmo contigo.
Negro é teu ventre,
porém macio.
E meus dedos capricham
sobre o aveludado relevo
das tatuagens.
Denso e morno é o luar,
cálido o cheiro húmido
do capim, acre o hálito
fundo da terra.
Venho cansado e tenho
fome de mulher. Sou branco.
Escolhi-te. Hoje durmo contigo:
Um ventre negro de mulher
arfando, a meu lado arfando,
o cansaço, o espasmo
e o sono. Nada mais.
Amanhã parto. E esqueço-te.
Depressa te esqueço.
    E teu ventre?

Mozambique

MULATTO

Rui Knopfli

I am a white man, I chose you.
Today I will sleep with you.
Black is your stomach
but it's so smooth
And my fingers play
on the velvety relief
on your tatoos.
Dense and warm is the moonlight
warm the humid smell of the grass, acrid
the heavy breathing of the earth.
I come to you tired and I hunger
for a woman. I am a white man.
I chose you. Today I will sleep with you:
A woman panting, panting at my side
your stomach black,
fatigue, spasm
then sleep. Nothing more.
Tomorrow I will go away. And I will forget you.
Quickly I will forget you.
        And in your womb?

Mozambique

ELEGIA A MAMANA ISABEL
que tinha 56 anos
quando morreu António Caetano

Rui Nogar

Os jornais o disseram
morreu António Caetano
velhíssimo velho colono.
Lutou por Moçambique
no tempo do Gungunhana.
Lutou por Portugal
durante a Grande Guerra.
Lutou e venceu.
Só agora foi vencido: morreu.

Os jornais o disseram
mas eu sei ah! dolorosamente eu sei
quem morreu não foi ele
foi mamana Isabel

quarenta e dois anos à sombra
da modesta reforma
do velhissimo velho colono
esboroaram-se naquele dia

quarenta e dois anos em que foram dois
dormindo comendo esperando
na frágil e velha cabana
do velhíssimo velho colono
senhor António Caetano

quarenta e dois anos
de luta   desespero   resignação

Mozambique

ELEGY FOR MAMANA ISABEL
Who was 56 years old
when António Caetano died

Rui Nogar

The newspapers announced it
António Caetano
the ancient old native of Portugal was dead.
He fought for Mozambique
in the time of Gungunhana.[1]
He fought for Portugal
in the Great War.
He fought and won.
Only now has he been defeated; he is dead.

The newspapers announced it
But oh how I know! How painfully I know
that he wasn't the one who died
it was mamana Isabel

Forty-two years living
on a modest pension
of the ancient old native of Portugal
came crumbling down on that day

forty-two years they were together
sleeping, eating, hoping
in the run-down old hut
of the ancient old native of Portugal
Mr. António Caetano

forty-two years
of struggle, despair, resignation

Mozambique

quarenta e dois anos
ah! quarenta e dois anos se foram
quando morreu António Caetano
velhissimo velho colono.

Mozambique

forty-two years
ah! forty-two years together
when António Caetano died
the ancient old native of Portugal.

1. A nineteenth century leader of the Batua in Mozambique who fought the Portuguese; for religious reasons he refused to use firearms. He was captured by the Portuguese and exiled to the Azores in 1896.

Mozambique

POEMA NA CHUVA

Glória de Sant'Anna

Por dentro da chuva tranquila e inúmera
as gotejantes acácias rubras,
cheias de flores e poemas húmidos
(dentro da chuva, bebendo a chuva).

Erguidas na água serena e rápida
as cheias de beleza acácias rubras,
mostrando antigas e álacres músicas
(de ignotes versos por sob a chuva).

"Se eu morrer longe sepulta-me no mar
dentro das algas ignorantes e lúcidas",
mas guarda, envolve meu coração intacto
junto à raiz das acácias rubras.

Mozambique

POEM ON RAIN

Glória de Sant'Anna

Veil of gentle rain
drops falling on red acacias
flowering into liquid poems
(petals wet from drinking rain).

Beads of water cling to branches
torrents of beauty, acacias in red,
revealing old cheerful melodies wed
(to imagined verses beneath falling rain).

"If I die far off, bury me at sea
wrapped in seaweed ignorant and clear,"
but keep my heart near
roots of red acacias.

Mozambique

DIA 7

Mutimati Barnabé João

No dia 7
Morreu uma camarada que vai ficar insepulta
Que vai tornar o ar perfumado e morreu
Que vai dar sempre flor de coragem e está morta
Que era da família nossa e ninguém vai chorar
Que os camaradas sabiam importante mas ela não
E via ficar insepulta orque é um grande cadáver
E não há terra suficiente para cavar esta sepultura.

É assim mesmo
Quando alguém cresce até ao tamanho do Povo
Fica por enterrar porque é muito grande.
O Herói não tem sepultura.

Mozambique

DAY 7

Mutimati Barnabé João

On day 7
A camarada died - she will be left unburied
She will perfume the air - and she is dead
She will always offer the flower of courage - and she is dead
She was one of us yet no one will cry
She was considered important by other camaradas but not by herself
And she will be left unburied because her dead body is too great
And there is no ground sufficient to hold her.

Thus it is
When someone grows to become the size of the People
That person cannot be buried, that person is too large
Heroes do not lie in the grave.

Mozambique

EU, O POVO

Mutimati Barnabé João

Eu, o Povo
Conheço a força da terra que rebenta a granda do grão
Fiz desta força um amigo fiel.

O vento sopra com força
A água corre com força
O fogo arde com força

Nos meus bracos que vão crescer vou estender panos de vela
Para agarrar o vento e levar a força do vento à Produção.
As minhas mãos vão crescer até fazerem pás de roda
Para agarrar a força da água e pô-la na Produção
Os meus pulmões vão crescer soprando na forja do coração
Para agarrar a força do fogo na Produção.

Eu, o Povo
Vou aprender a lutar do lado da Natureza
Vou ser camarada de armas dos quatro elementos.

A táctica colonialista é deixar o Povo no natural
Fazendo do Povo um inimigo da Natureza.

Eu, o Povo Moçambicano
Vou conhecer as minhas Grandes Forças todas.

Mozambique

I, THE PEOPLE

Mutimati Barnabé João

I, the People
I am acquainted with grenades of grain that explode with energy over the earth.

Wind blows with energy
Water races with energy
Fire burns with energy

With my arms that continue to expand I will unfurl sails
To catch the wind and use the wind's energy for Productivity.
My hands will expand until they become norias
To harness the energy of water and use it for Productivity.
My lungs will expand blowing into the forge of my heart
To use the energy of fire for Productivity.

I, the People
I will learn to struggle on the side of Nature
I will be comrade-in-arms with the four elements.

It is the colonialist tactic to leave the People ignorant
Making the People an enemy of Nature.

I, the Mozambican people
I will become acquainted with all my Great Strength and Power and Energy.

Mozambique

CARTA DE UM COMBATENTE

Jorge Rebelo

Mãe
eu tenho uma espingarda de ferro!

O teu filho,

Aquele a quem um dia tu viste
acorrentarem
(e choraste,
como se as correntes prendessem
e ferissem
as tuas mãos e os teus pés) —
O tau filho já é livre, mãe!
O teu filho tem uma espingarda de ferro.

A minha espingarda
vai quebrar todas as correntes,
via abrir todas as prisões,
vai matar todos os tiranos,
vai restituir a terra ao nosso povo.

Mãe, é belo lutar pela liberdade!
Há uma mensagem de justiça em cada bala que disparo,
há sonhos antigos que acordam como pássaros.

Nas horas de combate, na frente de batalha
a tua imagem próxima desce sobre mim.

É por ti também que eu luto, mãe!
Para que não haja lagrimas
nos teus olhos.

1977

Mozambique

LETTER FROM A COMBATANT

Jorge Rebelo

Mother
I carry a rifle of iron!

Your son
He whom one day you saw
in chains
(and you cried
as if the chains bound
and tore into the skin of
your wrists and your ankles) -
Your son is now free, mother!
Your son carries a rifle of iron.

My rifle
will rip asunder all the chains
will open all the prisons
will kill all the tyrants
will return the land to our people.

Mother, it is beautiful to fight for freedom!
There is a message of justice in each bullet I shoot,
there are old dreams awakening like birds.

In moments of combat, on the front line
your image comes to me.

And I am fighting for you too, mother!
So that you should not have tears
in your eyes.

1977

Mozambique

LIBERDADE

Jorge Rebelo

Liberdade,
tu hás-de chegar um dia
eu sei.
Se vieres tarde,
para além do meu tempo de luta e de conquista,
não te esqueças
que eu te amei
universalmente
e te busquei sem desânimo
durante toda a minha
               ignota
                      permanência.

Detém-te pois um instante
à beira do meu túmulo:
morto embora, eu saberei sentir-te
e conhecer-te
e remorrer
            então
                    tranquilamente.

1967

Mozambique

LIBERTY

Jorge Rebelo

Liberty,
you must come one day
I am sure.
If you come late
after my time of struggle and conquest
do not forget
that I loved you
universally
and I looked for you without being discouraged
during my life of
    anonymous
        perseverance.

Pause a moment
beside my grave:
although dead, I will still be aware of you
and recognize you
and then I will die a second death
    and finally
        rest in peace.

1967

Mozambique

JOSINA

Jorge Rebelo

Era ainda madrugada quando tu partiste.
Não tivemos tempo de dizer-te adeus —
partiste subitamente
silenciosamente
como uma estrela que se apaga.
Ninguém soube que partiste
senão por uma arma que ficou sem dono,
uma criança que chorou na noite.
Era ainda madrugada quando tu partiste.

Chorar-te?
É ainda cedo para te chorarmos.
A ausência fere
em função do tempo
e da compreensão.
Ontem estavas connosco
juntos construíamos o nosso mundo
Acarinhavas as crianças que a revolução
colocou ao teu cuidado
Transportavas contigo
        e espalhavas

o gesto e o fruto
da liberdade.
Hoje já não estás
— nao estas para sempre —
o que quer isto dizer?
Ah não serem as nossas mãos
martelos pesados
que batessem e rasgassem a terra
para tu saíres!

A nossa razão conhece a tua ausência
mas o nosso coração
recusa-se a compreender
e a aceitar.
É ainda cedo para te chorarmos.

Mozambique

JOSINA

Jorge Rebelo

It was still dawn when you departed.[1]
We didn't have time to say good-by to you -
you left suddenly
silently
like a shooting star whose fire dies in the sky.
There was no evidence that you had left
except for a weapon left without an owner.
a child crying in the night.
It was still dawn when you departed.

Weep over you?
It is too soon for us to weep over you.
Pain that results from loss
hurts more deeply as time passes
and we realize what has been taken from us.
Yesterday you were with us
together we were constructing our world
you were stroking the heads of children that the revolution
placed in your care.
You were carrying with you
    and you were scattering
the gesture and the fruit
of liberty.
Today you are no longer here
— and for eternity you will not be here —

What does it all mean?
Ah, might not our hands be
hammers
to beat and scratch the earth
so that you might come back to us!
Reason tells us you have gone
but our heart
refuses to understand
and accept it.
It is too soon for us to weep over you.

Mozambique

Aprenderemos nós a viver sem ti?
Quem nos dará as palavras certas
que curam e acalentam
nos nossos momentos
humanos
de hesitação e incerteza?

Quem encinará ao mundo a força
a coragem e a graça
das mulheres da nossa terra?
Eras p'ra nós a pureza,
a irmã, a camarada,
a revolução feita certeza.
Quando partiste, a razão de ser
de muita coisa
deizou de ser tão clara...

Mas escuta:
Quando a luta nos disser: — Avante!
nós avançaremos.
Mas tu irás também.
Nas nossas marchas, nos combates,
nas escolas, nas machambas,
em todas as missões
tu estarás connosco.
A tua juventude

interrompida aos 25 anos
será eterna
inspirando-nos, encorajando-nos.

Não, não precisamos aprender
a viver sem ti.
Continuamos
contigo
a nossa luta.

1971

Mozambique

Will we learn to go on living without you?
Who will speak to us and comfort us
and provide warmth and confidence
in our very human
moments
of doubt and uncertainty?

Who will show the world the strength
and courage and grace
of the women of our land?
You were for us purity,
a sister, a comrade,
total faith in the revolution.
When you departed, the raison d'être
of many things
no longer was so certain...

But listen:
When the struggle says to us: Forward, march!
we will go forward
But you will also go.
In our marches, in our combat,
in our schools, in our machambas[2]
in all our missions
you will be with us.
Your youth
interrupted at twenty-five
will live forever
inspiring us, encouraging us.

No, we do not need to learn
how to live without you.
With you
we continue
our struggle.

1971

1. Josina Machel, who died in 1971 from natural causes, was the wife of Samora Machel, the first President of The Peoples Republic of Mozambique.
2. A Mozambican word for "cultivated fields."

BIOGRAPHICAL NOTES

São Tomé and Príncipe

CAETANO DA COSTA ALEGRE was born on São Tomé in 1864 and died in Portugal in 1890. At the age of nineteen he went to Lisbon to continue his studies but he died young from tuberculosis. A journalist friend, Cruz de Magalhães, published a posthumous edition of his poems *Versos* in 1916.

FRANCISCO JOSÉ TENREIRO was born on São Tomé in 1921 and died in Lisbon in 1963. He studied in Portugal, where he earned his doctorate, as well as in England and taught geography at the University of Lisbon. He was Deputy for São Tomé and Príncipe in the National Assembly. In 1942 he published his major book of poems *Ilha de Nome Santo* and three years later published a study of North American literature. A complete volume of his poems appeared in 1967.

MARCELO VEIGA was born on Príncipe in 1892 and died there in 1976. He has lived both in Príncipe and Portugal. In 1959 he was imprisoned by the Portuguese state police, the PIDE, for his denouncing Portugal's economic policies towards her African colonies. He is considered the first negritude poet in Lusophone Africa. His first poem was published in 1921; he came to the attention of a wider audience when several of his poems were included in Alfredo Margarido's anthology *Poetas de São Tomé e Príncipe* (1963). A collection of about one hundred poems *Do negro para o negro*, edited by Manual Ferreira, is to be published in the near future.

Angola

JOAQUIM CORDEIRO DA MATTA was born in Icolo-e-Bengo in 1857 and died in Barra do Cuanza in 1894. His collection of poems *Delírios* was published in Lisbon in 1887. He was one of the first Angolans to er.courage the publication of stories and proverbs in African languages and to espouse the necessity for Angola to have its own literature. Self-taught, he wrote extensively--history, two novels, collections of Kimbundu folktales, a Kimbundu-

Portuguese dictionary, poetry. Unfortunately, many of his unpublished manuscripts have been lost.

GERALDO BESSA VICTOR, a lawyer living in Lisbon, was born in Luanda in 1917. He has published six volumes of poems including *Ecos Dispersos* (1941), *Mucanda* (1965), and *Monandengue* (1973). He has written numerous other works including a collection of short stories *Sanzala sem Batuque* (1967) and several books of essays on Angolan cultural and literary history. Gaston-Henry Aufrère translated a volume of selected poems into French under the title *Poèmes Africains*.

MÁRIO ANTÓNIO FERNANDES DE OLIVEIRA was born in Maquela do Zombo in 1934. One of the leading Angolan intellectuals studying in Lisbon in the early 1950s he won numerous awards for his poetry. An active participant in the furthering of Angolan literature through the publication of such journals as *Mensagem* and *Cultura*, he published his first of several volumes of poetry *Poemas* in 1956. Essayist, short story writer, literary historian and critic, he lives in Lisbon working in the international section of the Gulbenkian Foundation.

AGOSTINHO NETO was born in Catete in 1922 and died of cancer in Moscow in 1979. A medical doctor by training, and a political leader by calling, he led Angola to independence as President of MPLA (Popular Movement for the Liberation of Angola) and in 1975 became President. In his student years he was an activist on political and literary fronts. His volume of poems *Sagrada Esperança* was published first in Italian in Milan in 1963 and the first Portuguese edition came out in 1974. His poems have been published in many languages including English, Russian, Chinese, Swedish, French, and Serbo-Crotian.

ANTÓNIO JACINTO was born in Luanda in 1924. A combatant in the struggle for independence he was imprisoned for twelve years at Tarrafal in Cape Verde. His collection of poetry written during his confinement *Sobreviver em Tarrafal de Santiago* was awarded the Noma Prize for publishing in Africa in 1986. He is the first African poet to be so honored since the Noma Prize was inaugurated in 1979. He is also the first Lusophone writer in Africa to receive the Noma Prize. His poems have appeared in numerous anthologies and have been translated into other languages. His first collection *Poemas* was published in 1961. A former President of the Angolan Writers Union, he is at present retired.

ALDA LARA was born in Benguela in 1930 and died in Cambambe in 1962. While studying medicine in Portugal she became actively involved in the burgeoning Angolan literary activity publishing her poems in *Mensagem*. Her work appeared in various anthologies. A posthumous collection *Poemas* was published in Sá da Bandeira in 1966. After her death the Municipal Government of Sá da Bandeira instituted the Alda Lara Prize for poetry.

ANTERO ABREU was born in Luanda in 1927. A lawyer by profession and a movie critic as well, he has published poetry in various journals and newspapers and his work has appeared in various anthologies. His small collection of poems *A Tua Voz Angola* was published in Luanda in 1978.

FRANCISCO FERNANDO DA COSTA ANDRADE was born in Lépi in 1936. While a student in Lisbon in the early sixties he was director of Casa dos Estudantes do Império which published poetry by Africans. An active member of the MPLA he was imprisoned by the Dos Santos government in 1982 for an unflattering portrait of the Angolan President in his play *No velho ninguém toca*. His books of poetry include *Poesia Com Armas* (1975), *O País de Bissalanka* (1978), and *O Cunene Corre para o Sul* (1981).

ERNESTO LARA FILHO, brother of Alda Lara, was born in Benguela in 1932 and died in Huambo in 1977. A journalist in Luanda, he has been publishing poetry since the early 1960s He has published several collections of poems including *O Canto de Matrindinde* (1963) and *Seripipi na Gaiola* (1970).

JOFRE ROCHA (Roberto António Victor Francisco de Almeida) was born in Icolo e Bengo in 1951. He attended school in Luanda where he has worked as a bank clerk. Poet and short story writer he has published poems since 1959. His songs of the people and the revolution *Assim se Fez Madrugada* came out in 1977.

DAVID MESTRE was born in 1948. One of the leading journalists in Luanda, he moved to Angola with his family when he was only eight months old. In 1971 he established the group "Poesias-Hoje" which brought poetry readings, conferences, and plays to the large cities of Angola. He has been director of the literary section of the newspaper *A Palavra*. His publications include several volumes of poems, among them *Do Canto à Idade* (1977).

ARLINDO BARBEITOS, professor of history at the University of Lubango, was born in 1940. He has traveled widely in Europe and studied ethnology at the University of Frankfurt. His two volumes of poems *Angola Angolê Angolema* (1976) and *Nzoji* (1979) were published by Sá de Costa in Lisbon in their series of Angolan writers Colecção Vozes do Mundo.

CARLOS PIMENTEL was born in Moçamedes in 1944. He has worked in various jobs; presently he is director general of the publications house Empresa Nacional do Disco e de Publicações. His first published collection of poems *Tijolo a Tijolo* (1980) was awarded honorable mention by the jury of the Noma Prize.

JOÃO PEDRO was born in Namibia in 1948(?) and works in Luanda in the Ministry of Development. His collection of poems *Ponto de Situação* was published in 1978.

CARLOS FERREIRA was born in Luanda in 1959 and arranges programs for the Radio Nacional de Angola. His collection of poems *Projecto Comum* was published in 1981.

Cape Verde

JORGE BARBOSA was born in the city of Praia on the island of Santiago in 1902 and he died in Cova de Piedade, Portugal in 1971. He worked as a customs official for many years on the island of Sal. One of the founders of the journal *Claridade* in 1936, he published his first volume of poems *Arquipelago* in 1935. Other collections of poems include *Ambiente* (1941) and *Caderno de um ilhéu* (1956). His work has appeared in numerous journals and anthologies.

MANUEL LOPES, poet, short story writer, novelist, essayist, and painter, was born on the island of Santo Antão in 1907. He lives today in Lisbon. He worked for Western Telegraph on Cape Verde, the Azores, and later in Portugal. One of the founders of *Claridade*, he is equally noted for his two novels *Chuva Braba* (1956) and *Os Flagelados do Vento Leste* (1959). The latter has recently been made into the first major Cape Verdean movie. His short story "O Galo Cantou na Baia," written in 1936 marks the beginning of modern Cape Verdean prose. An interview with Manuel Lopes appears in *Wanasema-Conversations with African Writers* ed. Don Burness, (Athens: Ohio University, 1985).

OSVALDO ALCÃNTARA (poetic pseudonym of Baltasar Lopes da Silva) was born in Vila da Ribeira Brava on the island of São Nicolau in 1907. He lives today in Mindelo, São Vicente. A former teacher in the Liceu Gil Eanes (now called Liceu Ludgero Lima) in Mindelo, and a lawyer, he is most noted for his novel *Chiquinho* (1947). He has written several books on Cape Verdean culture and the crioule language of the islands. One of the creators of *Claridade*, he organized and edited the *Antologia da Ficção Cabo-Verdiana Contemporânea* in 1960; his collected poems *Cântico da Manhã Futura* was published in Praia in 1986.

YOLANDA MORAZZO was born in Mindelo, São Vicente in 1928. She studied in Portugal, France, and England and has taught French in Luanda, Angola, where some of her poems have been published. She lives in Lisbon.

GABRIEL MARIANO was born in Vila da Ribeira Brava on the island of São Nicolou in 1928. He went to school on São Vicente and later in Lisbon. He has lived in São Tomé, Mozambique, and Angola. Along with Jorge Pedro Barbosa he initiated the journal *Restauração*. He writes in both Portuguese and Crioulo. His works include two volumes of poems and two collections of stories. A retired judge, he lives in Queluz outside of Lisbon.

OVÍDIO MARTINS was born in Mindelo, São Vicente in 1928. While a student in Lisbon, he was arrested by the state police, the PIDE, for political activity. His poems have been published in Angola, Cape Verde, Brazil, Portugal, Algeria, Italy, and Belgium. One of the early Cape Verdean nationalists, he directly challenged in his poetry Portugal's political, economic, and psychological domination of Cape Verde. His most celebrated collection of poems *Gritarei Berrarei Matarei - Não Vou Para Pasárgada* was published in Holland in 1973.

ONÉSIMO SILVEIRA was born in Mindelo, São Vicente in 1935. He worked as a meteorologist in São Tomé in the late 1950s. An active member of the African Party for the Independence of Guiné and Cape Verde (PAIGC), he has lived in France, China, and Sweden, where he attended university. He has been a representative of Cape Verde at the United Nations. His most celebrated work, *Consciencialização na Literatura de Cabo Verde* (1963), calls for national consciousness raising. A book of his poems *Hora Grande* was published in Angola in 1962.

CORSINO FORTES was born in Mindelo in 1933. A former teacher, a lawyer, and Cape Verde's ambassador to Portugal, he has lived in Angola where he was a judge. His first book of poems *Pão e Fonema* was published in 1974. His work has appeared in such journals as *Boletim de Liceu Gil Eanes*, *Claridade*, and *Cabo Verde*.

ARMÉNIO VIEIRA was born in Praia in 1941. He has been a meteorologist and director of the Cape Verdean radio program *Tempo de Poesia*. His poems have been published in Cape Verde, Angola, and Portugal.

JOÃO RODRIGUES was born on the island of São Vicente in 1931. He lives in Mindelo where he works in the courthouse. The director of the small publishing house, Publicações Gráfica do Mindelo, he has written two short novels, *Casas e Casinhotos* (1981) and *O Casamento de Juquim Dadana* (1979), a travel book on his trip to the island of Brava, *O Jardim dos Rubros Cardeais* (1986), and *Pérolas do Sertão* (1986), a poem paying tribute to Cape Verdeans who emigrated.

LUIS ANDRADE SILVA (or LUIZ SILVA) was born in Mindelo in 1943 and emigrated to France in 1968. He established the first Cape Verdean Association in Paris. He is Director of the Center for Information for Emigrant Workers in Paris. His poems have been published in *Morabeza*, *Terra Nova*, and *Arquipelago*.

ANA JÚLIA MONTEIRO DE MACEDO SANÇA was born in Praia in 1949 and emigrated to Canada in 1981. She lives in Toronto where she works as a consular officer for the Consulate General of Portugal. She recently published her first book of poems *Arco Vírus e Vibra Sóis* (1986). Her poems have been published in *Arquipelago*, *Revista Alentejana*, and *Voz di Povo*.

Guiné Bissau

AMÍLCAR CABRAL was born in Bafatá in 1924. The son of Cape Verdean parents, he moved to Cape Verde with his family in 1931. He studied in Praia and then in Mindelo before going to Lisbon in 1945 to continue his studies in agronomy. The leader of the PAIGC he was murdered in Conakry in 1973. He wrote poems in the 1940s, a few of which were published in *Mensagem*. It was only after his death that a majority of his poems was discovered. A study of his poetry *Emergência da Poesia em Amílcar Cabral* by Oswaldo Osório was published in 1985(?).

CARLOS D'ALMADA was born in Bissau in 1957. He is the Director of Information and Political Activities in Guiné Bissau. His poems have appeared in journals in Portugal, Guiné Bissau, Grenada, and Cuba.

Mozambique

NOÉMIA DE SOUSA was born in 1927 in Maputo. She attended elementary school in Maputo and secondary school in Brazil. She lived for many years in Lisbon, but in 1964 she left Portugal for France. Her first poems were published in 1949 in *Itinerário* and *Vértice*. Her work has also appeared in *Présence Africaine* published in Paris and in nearly every anthology of Lusophone African poetry.

KALUNGANO (pseudonym of Marcelino dos Santos) was born in 1949 in Lumbo. Educated at the University of Lisbon and the Sorbonne, he was actively involved in the formation of the Front for the Liberation of Mozambique (FRELIMO) and in fact, was Vice-President of the party. He is currently Minister for Economic Planning. His poems have been translated into Russian and English. Two collections of poetry have been published in Russian in Moscow in 1959 and 1962.

JOSÉ CRAVEIRINHA was born in 1922 in Maputo. He has worked as a journalist for *O Brado Africano*, *Notícias*, and *Tribuna*. He was arrested in 1966 and held in Machava Prison. He works in the Library of the Economy at Eduardo Mondlane University in Maputo. His volumes of poems include *Chigubo* (1964), *Karingana ua Karingana* (1974) and *Maria* (1988).

RUI NOGAR was born in Maputo in 1935. The former secretary general of the Association of Mozambican Writers, he has contributed to major newspapers and literary journals in Mozambique including *O Brado Africano* and *Caliban*. His poems have appeared in anthologies in Portugal, Brazil, Moscow, and USA. His collection of poems *Silêncio Encancarado* was published in 1982.

RUI KNOPFLI was born in Inhambane in 1932. Journalist and literary critic, he was co-director of the journal *Caliban* with Grabato Dias. In 1975 he moved to London. His six volumes of poetry include *Reino Submarino* (1962), *Mangas Verdes con Sal* (1967), *A Ilha de Prospero* (1972), and *O Escriba Acocorado* (1978).

GLÓRIA DE SANT'ANNA was born in Lisbon in 1925 but lived and taught in Mozambique from 1951 to 1975. She was a regular contributor to *O Brado Africano*. She has written six books of poems including *Distância* (1951), *Livro de Água* (1961), and *Desde que o Mundo e 32 Poemas de Intervalo* (1972). In 1975 she published her first narrative work *Do Tempo Inutil*.

MUTIMATI BARNABÉ JOÃO refuses to reveal his identity. In his collection of poems *Eu, O Povo* (1975) he is described as an individual voice who belongs to the collective voice of the Mozambican people. It is not uncommon in Mozambique for poets to choose to be anonymous, for they believe that they are one with the people.

JORGE REBELO was born in Maputo in 1940. He went to Portugal where he attended the University of Coimbra. He was Secretary of Information for FRELIMO and edited *Mozambique Revolution*. He was Minister of Information in the Mozambican government after independence. His poems have been published in various anthologies published in Mozambique, Tanzania, Portugal, and the United States.

MONOGRAPHS IN INTERNATIONAL STUDIES

Africa Series

ISBN Prefix 0-89680-

25. Kircherr, Eugene C. ABBYSSINIA TO ZIMBABWE: A Guide to the Political Units of Africa in the Period 1947-1978. 1979. 3rd ed. 80pp.
100-4 $ 8.00*

27. Fadiman, Jeffrey A. MOUNTAIN WARRIORS: The Pre-Colonial Meru of Mt. Kenya. 1976. 82pp.
060-1 $ 4.75*

36. Fadiman, Jeffrey A. THE MOMENT OF CONQUEST: Meru, Kenya, 1907. 1979. 70pp.
081-4 $ 5.50*

37. Wright, Donald R. ORAL TRADITIONS FROM THE GAMBIA: Volume I, Mandinka Griots. 1979. 176pp.
083-0 $12.00*

38. Wright, Donald R. ORAL TRADITIONS FROM THE GAMBIA: Volume II, Family Elders. 1980. 200pp.
084-9 $15.00*

39. Reining, Priscilla. CHALLENGING DESERTIFICATION IN WEST AFRICA: Insights from Landsat into Carrying Capacity, Cultivation and Settlement Site Identification in Upper Volta and Niger. 1979. 180pp., illus.
102-0 $12.00*

41. Lindfors, Bernth. MAZUNGUMZO: Interviews with East African Writers, Publishers, Editors, and Scholars. 1981. 179pp.
108-X $13.00*

42. Spear, Thomas J. TRADITIONS OF ORIGIN AND THEIR INTERPRETATION: The Mijikenda of Kenya. 1982. xii, 163pp.
109-8 $13.50*

43. Harik, Elsa M. and Donald G. Schilling. THE POLITICS OF EDUCATION IN COLONIAL ALGERIA AND KENYA. 1984. 102pp.
117-9 $11.50*

44. Smith, Daniel R. THE INFLUENCE OF THE FABIAN COLONIAL BUREAU ON THE INDEPENDENCE MOVEMENT IN TANGANYIKA. 1985. x, 98pp.
125-X $ 9.00*

45. Keto, C. Tsehloane. AMERICAN-SOUTH AFRICAN RELATIONS 1784-1980: Review and Select Bibliography. 1985. 159pp.
128-4 $11.00*

46. Burness, Don, and Mary-Lou Burness, ed. WANASEMA: Conversations with African Writers. 1985. 95pp.
129-2 $ 9.00*

47. Switzer, Les. MEDIA AND DEPENDENCY IN SOUTH AFRICA: A Case Study of the Press and the Ciskei "Homeland". 1985. 80pp.
130-6 9.00*

48. Heggoy, Alf Andrew. THE FRENCH CONQUEST OF ALGIERS, 1830: An Algerian Oral Tradition. 1986. 101pp.
131-4 $ 9.00*

49. Hart, Ursula Kingsmill. TWO LADIES OF COLONIAL ALGERIA: The Lives and Times of Aurelie Picard and Isabelle Eberhardt. 1987. 156pp.
143-8 $9.00*

50. Voeltz, Richard A. GERMAN COLONIALISM AND THE SOUTH WEST AFRICA COMPANY, 1894-1914. 1988. 143pp.
146-2 $10.00*

51. Clayton, Anthony, and David Killingray. KHAKI AND BLUE: Military and Police in British Colonial Africa. 1989. 235pp.
147-0 $16.00*

52. Northrup, David. BEYOND THE BEND IN THE RIVER: African Labor in Eastern Zaire, 1865-1940. 1988. 195pp.
151-9 $12.00*

53. Makinde, M. Akin. AFRICAN PHILOSOPHY, CULTURE, AND TRADITIONAL MEDICINE. 1988. 175pp.
152-7 $11.00*

55. Burness, Don. A HORSE OF WHITE CLOUDS. 1989. 193pp.
158-6 $10.00*

Latin America Series

1. Frei, Eduardo M. THE MANDATE OF HISTORY AND CHILE'S FUTURE. Tr. by Miguel d'Escoto. Intro. by Thomas Walker. 1977. 79pp.
066-0 $ 8.00*

4. Martz, Mary Jeanne Reid. THE CENTRAL AMERICAN SOCCER WAR: Historical Patterns and Internal Dynamics of OAS Settlement Procedures. 1979. 118pp.
077-6 $ 8.00*

5. Wiarda, Howard J. CRITICAL ELECTIONS AND CRITICAL COUPS: State, Society, and the Military in the Processes of Latin American Development. 1979. 83pp.
082-2 $ 7.00*

6. Dietz, Henry A., and Richard Moore. POLITICAL PARTICIPATION IN A NON-ELECTORAL SETTING: The Urban Poor in Lima, Peru. 1979. viii, 102pp.
085-7 $ 9.00*

7. Hopgood, James F. SETTLERS OF BAJAVISTA: Social and Economic Adaptation in a Mexican Squatter Settlement. 1979. xii, 145pp.
101-2 $11.00*

8. Clayton, Lawrence A. CAULKERS AND CARPENTERS IN A NEW WORLD: The Shipyards of Colonial Guayaquil. 1980. 189pp., illus.
103-9 $15.00*

9. Tata, Robert J. STRUCTURAL CHANGES IN PUERTO RICO'S ECONOMY: 1947-1976. 1981. xiv, 104pp.
    107-1 $11.75*

10. McCreery, David. DEVELOPMENT AND THE STATE IN REFORMA GUATEMALA, 1871-1885. 1983. viii, 120pp.
    113-6 $ 8.50*

11. O'Shaughnessy, Laura N., and Louis H. Serra. CHURCH AND REVOLUTION IN NICARAGUA. 1986. 118pp.
    126-8 $11.OO*

12. Wallace, Brian. OWNERSHIP AND DEVELOPMENT: A Comparison of Domestic and Foreign Investment in Columbian Manufacturing. 1987. 186pp.
    145-4 $12.00*

13. Henderson, James D. CONSERVATIVE THOUGHT IN LATIN AMERICA: The Ideas of Laureano Gomez. 1988. 150pp.
    148-9 $11.00*

14. Summ, G. Harvey, and Tom Kelly. THE GOOD NEIGHBORS: America, Panama, and the 1977 Canal Treaties. 1988. 135pp.
    149-7 $11.00*

Southeast Asia Series

31. Nash, Manning. PEASANT CITIZENS: Politics, Religion, and Modernization in Kelantan, Malaysia. 1974. 181pp.
    018-0 $12.00*

38. Bailey, Conner. BROKER, MEDIATOR, PATRON, AND KINSMAN: An Historical Analysis of Key Leadership Roles in a Rural Malaysian District. 1976. 79pp.
    024-5 $7.00*

40. Van der Veur, Paul W. FREEMASONRY IN INDONESIA FROM RADERMACHER TO SOEKANTO, 1762-1961. 1976. 37pp.
    026-1 $4.00*

43. Marlay, Ross. POLLUTION AND POLITICS IN THE PHILIPPINES. 1977. 121pp.
029-6 $7.00*

44. Collier, William L., et al. INCOME, EMPLOYMENT AND FOOD SYSTEMS IN JAVANESE COASTAL VILLAGES. 1977. 160pp.
031-8 $10.00*

45. Chew, Sock Foon and MacDougall, John A. FOREVER PLURAL: The Perception and Practice of Inter-Communal Marriage in Singapore. 1977. 61pp.
030-X $6.00*

47. Wessing, Robert. COSMOLOGY AND SOCIAL BEHAVIOR IN A WEST JAVANESE SETTLEMENT. 1978. 200pp.
072-5 $12.00*

48. Willer, Thomas F., ed. SOUTHEAST ASIAN REFERENCES IN THE BRITISH PARLIAMENTARY PAPERS, 1801-1972/73: An Index. 1978. 110pp.
033-4 $ 8.50*

49. Durrenberger, E. Paul. AGRICULTURAL PRODUCTION AND HOUSEHOLD BUDGETS IN A SHAN PEASANT VILLAGE IN NORTHWESTERN THAILAND: A Quantitative Description. 1978. 142pp.
071-7 $9.50*

50. Echauz, Robustiano. SKETCHES OF THE ISLAND OF NEGROS. 1978. 174pp.
070-9 $10.00*

51. Krannich, Ronald L. MAYORS AND MANAGERS IN THAILAND: The Struggle for Political Life in Administrative Settings. 1978. 139pp.
073-3 $ 9.00*

54. Ayal, Eliezar B., ed. THE STUDY OF THAILAND: Analyses of Knowledge, Approaches, and Prospects in Anthropology, Art History, Economics, History and Political Science. 1979. 257pp.
079-2 $13.50*

56. Duiker, William J. VIETNAM SINCE THE FALL OF SAIGON. Updated edition. 1989. 322pp.
133-0 $14.00*

57. Siregar, Susan Rodgers. ADAT, ISLAM, AND CHRISTIANITY IN A BATAK HOMELAND. 1981. 108pp.
110-1 $10.00*

58. Van Esterik, Penny. COGNITION AND DESIGN PRODUCTION IN BAN CHIANG POTTERY. 1981. 90pp.
078-4 $12.00*

59. Foster, Brian L. COMMERCE AND ETHNIC DIFFERENCES: The Case of the Mons in Thailand. 1982. x, 93pp.
112-8 $10.00*

60. Frederick, William H., and John H. McGlynn. REFLECTIONS ON REBELLION: Stories from the Indonesian Upheavals of 1948 and 1965. 1983. vi, 168pp.
111-X $ 9.00*

61. Cady, John F. CONTACTS WITH BURMA, 1935-1949: A Personal Account. 1983. x, 117pp.
114-4 $ 9.00*

62. Kipp, Rita Smith, and Richard D. Kipp, eds. BEYOND SAMOSIR: Recent Studies of the Batak Peoples of Sumatra. 1983. viii, 155pp.
115-2 $ 9.00*

63. Carstens, Sharon, ed. CULTURAL IDENTITY IN NORTHERN PENINSULAR MALAYSIA. 1986. 91pp.
116-0 $ 9.00*

64. Dardjowidjojo, Soenjono. VOCABULARY BUILDING IN INDONESIAN: An Advanced Reader. 1984. xviii, 256pp.
118-7 $26.00*

65. Errington, J. Joseph. LANGUAGE AND SOCIAL CHANGE IN JAVA: Linguistic Reflexes of Modernization in a Traditional Royal Polity. 1985. xiv, 198pp.
120-9 $12.00*

66. Binh, Tran Tu. THE RED EARTH: A Vietnamese Memoir of Life on a Colonial Rubber Plantation. Tr. by John Spragens. Ed. by David Marr. 1985. xii, 98pp.
119-5 $ 9.00*

67. Pane, Armijn. SHACKLES. Tr. by John McGlynn. Intro. by William H. Frederick. 1985. xvi, 108pp.
122-5 $ 9.00*

68. Syukri, Ibrahim. HISTORY OF THE MALAY KINGDOM OF PATANI. Tr. by Conner Bailey and John N. Miksic. 1985. xx, 98pp.
123-3 $10.50*

69. Keeler, Ward. JAVANESE: A Cultural Approach. 1984. xxxvi, 523pp.
121-7 $18.00*

70. Wilson, Constance M., and Lucien M. Hanks. BURMA-THAILAND FRONTIER OVERSIXTEEN DECADES: Three Descriptive Documents. 1985. x, 128pp.
124-1 $10.50*

71. Thomas, Lynn L., and Franz von Benda-Beckmann, eds. CHANGE AND CONTINUITY IN MINANGKABAU: Local, Regional, and Historical Perspectives on West Sumatra. 1986. 363pp.
127-6 $14.00*

72. Reid, Anthony, and Oki Akira, eds. THE JAPANESE EXPERIENCE IN INDONESIA: Selected Memoirs of 1942-1945. 1986. 411pp., 20 illus.
132-2 $18.00*

73. Smirenskaia, Zhanna D. PEASANTS IN ASIA: Social Consciousness and Social Struggle. Tr. by Michael J. Buckley. 1987. 248pp.
134-9 $12.50

74. McArthur, M.S.H. REPORT ON BRUNEI IN 1904. Ed. by A.V.M. Horton. 1987. 304pp.
135-7 $13.50

75. Lockard, Craig Alan. FROM KAMPUNG TO CITY. A Social History of Kuching Malaysia 1820-1970. 1987. 311pp.
   136-5 $14.00*

76. McGinn, Richard. STUDIES IN AUSTRONESIAN LINGUISTICS. 1988. 492pp.
   137-3 $18.50*

77. Muego, Benjamin N. SPECTATOR SOCIETY: The Philippines Under Martial Rule. 1988. 232pp.
   138-1 $12.50*

78. Chew, Sock Foon. ETHNICITY AND NATIONALITY IN SINGAPORE. 1987. 229pp.
   139-X $12.50*

79. Walton, Susan Pratt. MODE IN JAVANESE MUSIC. 1987. 279pp.
   144-6 $12.00*

80. Nguyen Anh Tuan. SOUTH VIETNAM TRIAL AND EXPERIENCE: A Challenge for Development. 1987. 482pp.
   141-1 $15.00*

81. Van der Veur, Paul W., ed. TOWARD A GLORIOUS INDONESIA: Reminiscences and Observations of Dr. Soetomo. 1987. 367pp.
   142-X $13.50*

82. Spores, John C. RUNNING AMOK: An Historical Inquiry. 1988. 190pp.
   140-3 $13.00*

83. Tan Malaka. FROM JAIL TO JAIL. Tr. and ed. by Helen Jarvis. 1989. 3 vols. 1200pp.
   150-0 $45.00*

84. Devas, Nick. FINANCING LOCAL GOVERNMENT IN INDONESIA. 1989. 344pp.
   153-5 $14.00*

85. Suryadinata, Leo. MILITARY ASCENDANCY AND POLITICAL CULTURE: A Study of Indonesia's Golkar. 1989. 222pp.
179-9 $11.50*

86. Williams, Michael. COMMUNISM, RELIGION, AND REVOLT IN BANTEN. 1989. 314pp.
155-1 $14.00*

ORDERING INFORMATION

Orders for titles in the Monographs in International Studies series should be placed through the Ohio University Press/Scott Quadrangle/ Athens, Ohio 45701-2979. Individuals must remit pre-payment via check, VISA, MasterCard, CHOICE, or American Express. Individuals ordering from the United Kingdom, Continental Europe, Middle East, and Africa should order through Academic and University Publishers Group, 1 Gower Street, London WC1E 6HA, England. Other individuals ordering from outside of the U.S., please remit in U.S. funds by either International Money Order or check drawn on a U.S. bank. Postage and handling is $2.00 for the first book and $.50 for each additional book. Prices and availability are subject to change without notice.

PQ 9906.5 .E5 H67 1989

A Horse of white clouds

DATE DUE

DEC 0 8 1992		

WITHDRAWN from the Alma College Library

HIGHSMITH 45-220